AF677829

THE NEW EUROPEAN PATENT

On 17 December 2012, following a complex negotiation which lasted 12 years, the European Parliament adopted Regulations (EU) 1257/2012 and 1260/2012 and the text of the Agreement on a Unified Patent Court (UPC Agreement). These instruments institute the 'European patent with unitary effect', the first unified system for the protection of inventions within the European Union. The two Regulations will be applicable after the entry into force of the UPC Agreement, which was signed on 19 February 2013 by 24 Member States of the European Union.

This book traces the evolution of the idea behind the institution of the European patent with unitary effect, including a comparative analysis of the existing parallel regional and international procedures for the protection of inventions. It presents a synthesis of the different phases of the negotiations which led to the adoption of the first unitary patent system within the European Union. In addition it examines the provisions of the two Regulations, of the UPC Agreement and of the jurisdictional system under Brussels I Regulation. Finally, the Appendix contains the text of Regulations (EU) 1257 and 1260/2012 and of the UPC Agreement.

The New European Patent

Alfredo Ilardi

·HART·
PUBLISHING
OXFORD AND PORTLAND, OREGON
2015

Published in the United Kingdom by Hart Publishing Ltd
16C Worcester Place, Oxford, OX1 2JW
Telephone: +44 (0)1865 517530
Fax: +44 (0)1865 510710
E-mail: mail@hartpub.co.uk
Website: http://www.hartpub.co.uk

Published in North America (US and Canada) by
Hart Publishing
c/o International Specialized Book Services
920 NE 58th Avenue, Suite 300
Portland, OR 97213-3786
USA
Tel: +1 503 287 3093 or toll-free: (1) 800 944 6190
Fax: +1 503 280 8832
E-mail: orders@isbs.com
Website: http://www.isbs.com

© Alfredo Ilardi 2015

This book was originally published in Italian as *Il Nuovo Brevetto Europeo*
(Zanichelli, Bologna, 2013)

Alfredo Ilardi has asserted his right under the Copyright, Designs and Patents Act 1988, to be identified as the author of this work.

Hart Publishing is an imprint of Bloomsbury Publishing plc.

All rights reserved. No part of this publication may be reproduced, stored in a retrieval system, or transmitted, in any form or by any means, without the prior permission of Hart Publishing, or as expressly permitted by law or under the terms agreed with the appropriate reprographic rights organisation. Enquiries concerning reproduction which may not be covered by the above should be addressed to Hart Publishing Ltd at the address above.

British Library Cataloguing in Publication Data
Data Available

ISBN: 978-1-84946-833-6

Typeset by Compuscript Ltd, Shannon
Printed and bound in Great Britain by
CPI Group (UK) Ltd, Croydon CR0 4YY

PREFACE

It is known by those who study the genesis and the dynamic of international relations that after the conclusion of the Uruguay Round (Geneva, 1986–94), the multilateral activities of states with respect to the conclusion of international agreements have undergone a substantial reduction so that, in perspective, this Round can well be considered to be the last example of a successful global multilateral negotiation. It should be added that in a period characterised by the increasing interdependence of states from economic, commercial and financial perspectives, the contraction in the volume of intergovernmental multilateral cooperation has unexpectedly left new gaps in the system of bilateral negotiations, to such an extent that it is possible to conceive of a gradual abandonment of multilateral practice in international relations. And it is interesting to note in this respect that, on the contrary, at the end of the nineteenth century, in a climate of confrontation among countries both in terms of the assertion of national identities and in the expansion of national boundaries, states were actively exploring the possibility of reaching multilateral understandings, which would 'multiplicate' and play a fundamental role on the international scene in the following century.

In the framework of existing regional economic integration agreements, as in the case of those establishing the European Union (EU), the increasing lack of a predisposition towards intergovernmental multilateral initiatives has determined a complex and contradictory devolution of the European integration project, represented by individual attempts by Member States to reclaim national prerogatives in specific areas. A good example of this devolutional tendency has been the long and complex negotiation process for the creation of a unitary system for the protection of inventions within the EU, which after 12 years led to the adoption of two Regulations and an international Agreement,[1] a positive, though long-awaited, conclusion which necessitated recourse to the exceptional measure of 'enhanced cooperation' in order to overcome the impossibility of reaching complete consensus.

In examining the elaborate normative system created by the European patent with unitary effect, there were three principal aims. The first was to trace the origin and evolution of the idea behind the creation of a unitary patent system

[1] Regulation (EU) No 1257/2012 of the European Parliament and the Council of 17 December 2012 implementing enhanced cooperation in the area of unitary patent protection; Council Regulation (EU) No 1260/2012 of 17 December 2012 implementing enhanced cooperation in the area of unitary patent protection with regard to applicable translation arrangements; Agreement on a Unified Patent Court and Statute of the Court of 19 February 2013.

within the EU in the framework of the parallel developments which took place at the international and regional levels in the field of the protection of inventions. From this perspective, we thought that it was important to place the decision to complete the EU industrial property infrastructure, after the adoption of common rules on trademarks and industrial designs, in the pertinent international and regional normative context within which this idea was born and evolved.

The second aim was to offer a summary of the different phases of the negotiations which started with the Council decision at the Lisbon meeting on 24 March 2000, opening the way up to the creation of the Community patent. We considered it useful and appropriate to contribute to the creation of the historic memory of this long negotiation because we think that the important result obtained cannot be properly appreciated and valued without referring to the various stages of its process.

The third aim was to carry out an examination of the characteristics and content of the legal instruments which were adopted at the conclusion of the negotiations. We are fully aware that such an analysis should be regarded as preliminary, since only after the practical application of the adopted provisions and the establishment of a jurisprudence would it be possible to prepare a comprehensive commentary on these norms.

In conclusion, we hope that the synthesis of the three aspects of the unitary patent examined in this work will provide a 'reading' of the new European patent system, that will constitute a basis for future studies of this legal instrument, which qualifies as an essential element of the economic and technological development of the EU Member States.

I should like to express my sincere thanks to Dr Luigi Filippi, Presidency of the Council, Department of Community Policies, Rome, to Simona Šeikytè and Andrea Leisenfeld, European Commission, Directorate General for the Internal Market and Services, D2, Industrial Property, Brussels, and to Stefan Luginbuehl, International Legal Affairs, PCT, Dir. 5.2.2, European Patent Office, Munich, for their cooperation and kindness in supplying me with information and documentation.

Particular thanks go to Veronique Orlando, WIPO, Geneva, who assisted me with her usual competence in the preparation of the final text of the manuscript.

CONTENTS

LIST OF ABBREVIATIONS

CPC	Community Patent Convention
EC	European Community
ECJ	European Court of Justice
EEC	European Economic Community
EFTA	European Free Trade Association
EPC	European Patent Convention
EPC 2000	European Patent Convention (revised by Act of 29 November 2000)
EPLA	European Patent Litigation Agreement
EPO	European Patent Organisation
EU	European Union
GATT	General Agreement on Tariffs and Trade
IPC	International Patent Classification
OECD	Organisation for Economic Co-operation and Development
OHIM	Office for Harmonization in the Internal Market
PCT	Patent Cooperation Treaty
SMEs	Small and medium-sized enterprises
TEC	Treaty Establishing the European Community
TEU	Treaty on European Union
TFEU	Treaty on the Functioning of the European Union
TRIPS	Agreement on Trade-Related Aspects of Intellectual Property Rights
UN	United Nations
UNCTAD	United Nations Conference on Trade and Development
UPC	Unified Patent Court
WIPO	World Intellectual Property Organization
WTO	World Trade Organization

AUTHOR'S NOTE

For the text and the summary of the intellectual property treaties cited in this work, see A Ilardi and M Blakeney, *The International Encyclopaedia of Intellectual Property Treaties* (Oxford, Oxford University Press, 2004).

1

Innovation and the Industrial Property Protection Systems in the European Union

I. The Genesis of Innovation

Beyond the various theoretical elaborations which have tried to establish what should be understood by the term 'innovation',[1] it can be said that the attitude to innovate is embedded in the nature of the human being and measures its evolution. To innovate means, above all, to modify, to change. In particular, it means to modify an existing system—irrespective of how primitive it may be—composed of several interacting elements with the aim of obtaining a certain result, introducing one or more new elements which simplify and improve the securing of that result. The subsequent consolidation of these new elements and their new interaction generates knowledge which constitutes the basis for further changes, thus evolving into innovation, in a theoretical infinite process.

If these concepts are transferred from a pure theoretical dimension into the reality of the modern associative life, we note that the enterprise is, at the same time, the principal driving power and the principal beneficiary of the innovative process, being, on the one hand, at the root of such process and, on the other, benefiting from its results. In a contemporary industrial and commercial framework, the innovation process may have different origins, expressions and functions. It may be, for example, the result of a programmed research directed at achieving some specific results, or the consequence of the conversion of production or commercial systems already in use. It may consist in the re-designing of existing products applying new technologies or in the creation of new commercial, marketing or organisational patterns with a view to improving the competitive position of the enterprise.

Innovation constitutes an essential incentive of the economic development because of its capacity to stimulate development among the competition, so that

[1] Out of the extensive bibliography on innovation, see in general the works of Alfred Marshall (1842–1924) and of Joseph Schumpeter (1833–1950). More recently, John K Galbraith (1908–2006) has dedicated several enlightening considerations on the concept of innovation.

its impact in the general economy has an amplifying effect. The economic value of industrial and commercial activity incorporating innovative elements increases, thus encouraging the emergence of new enterprises. In this perspective, the development, use and divulgation of new production and commercial methods becomes a dynamic element of the innovative process.

II. Patent Protection as an Incentive to Innovation

In principle, the results of any innovative process can be protected under the patent system. However, in order to be protectable, they must conform to the rules on patentability provided for in a uniform way by most of the national laws on the protection of inventions. The three fundamental rules for the protection of inventions are novelty, inventive activity and the industrial application of the subject matter to be protected. An invention is considered to be 'new' if, before the filing of the relevant patent application, it was not already known to the general public. For 'inventive activity', it is understood that the invention must be unexpectedly original, so as to represent a non-evident progress in the framework of the technological field to which the invention belongs. The requirement of 'industrial application' means that the invention must be fully applicable in the industrial field. In this context, the notion of industry should be understood in its largest sense.

We wanted to recall briefly the general requisites of patentability to underline the principle that the results of the innovative activity are not protected as such by the patent system, but that in order to be protectable, they must have certain specific characteristics.

Notwithstanding the fact that the patent system offers the innovation the most comprehensive form of protection, the lack of one or more of these requirements does not exclude the possibility that an innovative result could be protected, depending on the nature of the innovation, under the legal rules governing other forms of protection of industrial property, such as utility models, industrial designs, trademarks and trade names.

It is the general opinion today that the norms on patents govern an ad hoc relationship between the inventor and society, by which the former receives ex ante the assurance that the result of his inventive activity will be exclusively protected for a given period of time. The main condition for the working of this assurance is that the inventor fully divulges his invention by way of a detailed description in the patent application, thus putting the inventive result obtained at the disposal of society. Once the protection period has elapsed, the invention enters into the public domain to the benefit of society in general and, in particular, of the specific technological field to which the invention belongs. This configuration contributes in reaching two objectives: it encourages, on the one hand, the innovative activity and, on the other hand, the disclosure of its results, two basic elements of economic and technological development.

The focal point of this approach, from the perspective of the originator of the innovative process (typically the enterprise), is the securing, through patent protection, of the exclusive faculty to exclude others from the working of the patent for the period of its validity. This faculty gives the owner of the patent the right to work the patented invention directly or authorise others to do so, for example, under licence. However, the exclusive right deriving from the grant of a valid patent should be understood not only as a means to prevent potential competitors from gaining access to protected innovations, but also as an incentive to look for and propose new advanced solutions. From this perspective, the patent system qualifies, on the one hand, as a warrant of the protection of the results of the innovative process and, on the other hand, as a primary incitement factor.[2]

The patent system does not exhaust its function in the private framework. From another viewpoint, it constitutes, together with other forms of direct public intervention, a valid instrument at the disposal of governments for the implementation of political choices relating to the development of technology at the national level. Comparing the role performed to this end by the patent system with that of other instruments, the conclusion was reached that patent protection not only encourages research, but favours the divulging of its protected results through commercialisation.[3]

III. The Systems of Industrial Property Protection within the European Union: The Community Trademark and the Community Industrial Design

Within the European Union (EU), the protection of industrial property—that is, for the purposes of this work, patents for invention, industrial designs and models, trademarks and service marks[4]—is governed by two complementary normative systems: by the national legislations of the Member States of the EU and by the applicable EU Regulations. Putting aside national legislation, the applicable EU Regulations cover trademarks and industrial designs. They consist, with respect to trademarks, of Council Regulation (EC) 40/94 of 20 December 1993

[2] See E Duguet and C Lelarge, 'Does Patenting Increases the Private Incentives to Innovate? A Microeconometric Analysis', Cahiers de la Maison des Sciences Economiques, Université Panthéon, Sorbonne, 2004. The authors reach the conclusion that the value of innovation is increased by patent protection.

[3] See the detailed analysis of D Guellec and B van Pottelsberghe de la Potterie, *The Economics of the European Patent System-IP Policy for Innovation and Competition* (Oxford, Oxford University Press, 2007).

[4] The Paris Convention for the Protection of Industrial Property specifies in its Article 1(2) that: 'The protection of industrial property has as its object patents, utility models, industrial designs, trademarks, service marks, trade names, indications of source or appellations of origin, and the repression of unfair competition.'

on the Community Trade Mark and, as far as industrial designs are concerned, of Council Regulation (EC) 6/2002 of 12 December 2001 on Community Designs. The two Regulations have established, respectively, the Community Trade Mark and Design[5] systems which are connected to the international registration systems in the field of trademarks and industrial designs administered by the World Intellectual Property Organization (WIPO), which has its headquarters in Geneva.

These systems are constituted by the Madrid Agreement Concerning the International Registration of Marks (1891), which was modified in 1979 and accompanied by the Protocol Relating to the Madrid Agreement (1989) and by the Hague Agreement Concerning the International Deposit of Industrial Designs (1925), which itself was modified by the Geneva Act (1999). The link between the Community Trade Mark and Design systems and the Madrid and the Hague Agreement systems has been made by two Council decisions which have approved the adhesion of the EU to the Protocol Relating to the Madrid Agreement[6] and to the Geneva Act of the Hague Agreement, respectively.[7] The framework of these instruments is completed[8] by the substantive provisions of the Agreement on the Trade-Related Aspects of Intellectual Property Rights (TRIPS) (1994), which resulted from the Agreement Establishing the World Trade Organization (WTO) at the conclusion of the negotiations of the Uruguay Round (1986–94) and by those of the Trademark Law Treaty (TLT) (1994), which was modified by the Singapore Act (2006) and administered by the WIPO.[9] Finally, mention should be made of two EU Directives[10] which aimed at aligning the national provisions on trademarks and industrial designs of the Member States in order to favour the creation of new innovative processes and the development of competition in the internal market.

The coordinated corpus of these norms has established, within the EU, a regional system of protection of distinctive signs and designs coexisting with those provided for under the national legislation of Member States. Through the links with the multilateral instruments administered by the WIPO, it extends its functions at the international level. Under this unified system, a trademark and a design owner can benefit from uniform protection across the entire territory of the EU through a single registration procedure at the Office for Harmonization in the Internal Market (OHIM), which is located in Alicante, Spain. The OHIM,

[5] On the Community Trade Mark, see: M Franzosi et al, *The European Community Trade Mark* (The Hague, Kluwer, 1997). On the Community Design, see: D Cohen, *Le droit des dessins et modèls: Droit français, droit communetaire et droit international* (Paris, Economica, 2009).

[6] Council Decision 2003/793/EU of 27 October 2003 and Council Regulation (EU) 1992/2003, which modifies Council Regulation (EU) 40/49 of 20 December 1993 on the Community Trade Mark to give effect to the adhesion of the EU to the Protocol to the Madrid Agreement.

[7] Council Decision 2006/954/EU of 18 December 2006 and Council Regulation (EU) 1891/2006 of 18 December 2006, which gives effect to the adhesion of the EU to the Geneva Act of the Hague Agreement.

[8] Council Regulation (EU) 3288/94 of 22 December 1994.

[9] The EU has been a contracting party of the Trademark Law Treaty since 30 June 1995.

[10] Council Directive 89/104/EU of 21 December 1988 and Directive 98/71/EU of the Parliament and of the Council of 13 October 1998.

which administers the registration procedures for the Community Trade Mark and Design systems, plays, at the same time, a substantial role in the harmonisation of the national procedures and in the coordination of the activities of the industrial property offices of the Member States. Because of the links with the international registration systems administered by the WIPO, the owners of Community Trade Marks and Designs may ask for the international protection of their titles and, likewise, the owners of international registrations may obtain protection for their registrations under the Community Trade Mark and Design system. This enlarged flexible legal framework gives users the option to chose, separately or in combination with others, several ways to secure protection of his distinctive signs or designs. These are not methods, but three alternative 'routes' to secure protection: the one under national law; that under the Community Trade Mark and Design systems; and the international one under the instruments administered by the WIPO.

IV. The Lack of a Unitary Patent System within the EU

Unitary norms in the field of patents for invention, like the Community Trade Mark and Design systems, do not exist yet in the context of the EU. However, as we will see in the subsequent chapters, after more than a decade of complex negotiations, a unitary patent and jurisdictional system has been set up in the EU. Until the entry into force of these unitary norms, the provisions of the European Patent Convention (EPC 1973)[11] applied and will continue to apply as far as the protection of inventions is concerned. This multilateral treaty, which is in force in 38 states,[12] including the 28 Member States of the EU, has established a regional system for the protection of inventions, providing for a unified procedure for the granting of a 'European patent' which has the same effects as a national patent in each State Party to the EPC. As regards the procedures for the filing of a patent application, at the same time, in several countries that are not State Parties to the EPC, EU Member States may benefit from the simplified procedures provided for by the Patent Cooperation Treaty (PCT) (1970), since they are also State Parties to the PCT. This international instrument, administered by the WIPO, interacts with the EPC, extending its scope at the international level. The EPC and the PCT, respectively, have deployed and currently deploy, with success, a primary harmonising function of the national legislation of their respective Member States and, within the EU, have filled the gap created by the lack of a unitary system for the protection of inventions.

[11] The official title of the EPC is the Convention on the Grant of European Patents.

[12] Albania, Austria, Belgium, Bulgaria, Croatia, the Czech Republic, Cyprus, Denmark, Estonia, Finland, France, Germany, Greece, Hungary, Iceland, Ireland, Italy, Latvia, Liechtenstein, Lithuania, Luxembourg, Macedonia, Malta, Monaco, the Netherlands, Norway, Poland, Portugal, Romania, San Marino, Serbia, Slovakia, Slovenia, Spain, Sweden, Switzerland, Turkey and the UK. The following EPC Member States are not members of the EU: Albania, Iceland, Liechtenstein, the Former Yugoslav Republic of Macedonia, Monaco, Norway, San Marino, Serbia, Switzerland and Turkey.

2

Towards the Establishment of an Integrated European Patent System for the Protection of Inventions

I. First Attempts at the International Harmonisation of National Patent Legislations and Procedures

The study of multilateral relations in the field of industrial property, after the adoption in 1883 of the Paris Convention for the Protection of Industrial Property, shows that, contrary to what took place as far as distinctive signs, industrial designs and appellations of origin are concerned, the first attempts at harmonising the norms and national procedures relating to the protection of inventions started and yielded results only after the conclusion of the Second World War.[1] An explanation of this relatively late accomplishment can be found in the troubled history of the national European patent systems during the last decade of the nineteenth century, which in certain countries led to a 'crisis' of the patent system.[2]

This adverse climate determined in European countries a general reluctance to depart from well-established national norms and procedures in order to take part in multilateral negotiations with the aim of harmonising their respective patent systems or specific sectors of such systems. The spirit of compromise in pursuing uniform solutions, which characterised the negotiations for the adoption of the Paris Convention,[3] was missing in the attitude of national industrial property

[1] The first example of the simplification of national registration procedures in the field of industrial property took place with the conclusion on 14 April 1891 of the Madrid Agreement Concerning the International Registration of Marks, which is still in operation today. The Madrid Agreement inspired the preparation and the adoption of other registration agreements: the Hague Agreement for the International Deposit of Industrial Designs of 6 November 1925 and the Lisbon Agreement on the Protection of Appellations of Origin and their International Registration of 13 October 1958.

[2] See SP Ladas, *Patents, Trademarks and Related Right: National and International Protection* (Cambridge, MA, Harvard University Press, 1975) 284. The author points out that in 1896, the Netherlands abolished patent rights, that Switzerland adopted its first patent law only in 1888 and that, towards the end of the nineteenth century, industrial sectors in England, France and Germany were discussing the question of patent abuses and a possible consequential abolition of the patent system.

[3] See GHC Bodenhausen, *Guide to the Application of the Paris Convention for the Protection of Industrial Property, as Revised at Stockholm in 1967* (Geneva, BIRPI, 1968).

administrations. This attitude was motivated by the concern that an internationalisation of patent systems beyond the basic rules established by the Paris Convention would have exposed a country's industrial production and relevant 'know-how' to dangerous competition. Finally, the economic depression between the two World Wars and its negative repercussions on industrial development had encouraged the competent national authorities, supported by interested circles, to retain their respective national patent legislation laws.

With the general resumption of industrial production and of commercial activities during the so-called 'reconstruction period' following the end of the Second World War, the position of the European industrial property offices and of the industry started to change. On the one hand, national administrations had to face a substantial increase in terms of the difficulties they faced in administering their respective patent systems. This was the consequence of the constant growth in the number of patent applications and of requests for protection for increasingly complex inventive solutions. On the other hand, national patent legislation proved inadequate to supply the users of the patent system with appropriate responses to the problems posed by an economic and industrial context which was becoming rapidly international and which would have taken advantage from the harmonisation of national norms. Furthermore, new countries entering the international scene and looking to achieve parity with industrialised countries experienced technical difficulties and high costs in adopting forms of patent legislation which were comparable with those in force in the majority of more advanced countries.

All these elements combined to favour the emergence of a more flexible approach to the question of harmonising national laws with a view to simplifying and rationalising access to the protection of inventions. This new tendency developed in Europe between 1947 and 1963 and led to the adoption of the first international agreements in the field of patents.[4] Upon the initiative of France and the three Benelux countries (Belgium, Luxembourg and the Netherlands), on 6 June 1947, the Treaty Establishing the International Patent Institute was adopted at The Hague. The aim of the Treaty was to substitute the different novelty examinations carried out on patent applications by the administration of each participating state with a single examination made by a common organisation. This treaty was followed by two agreements, both established under the auspices of the Council of Europe: the European Convention Relating to the Formalities Required for Patent Applications of 11 December 1953 and the Convention on the Unification of Certain Points of Substantive Law on Patents of Invention of 27 November 1963.

[4] Outside Europe, one of the first regional agreements in the field of industrial property—the Libreville Agreement on the Creation of an African and Malgasy Office of Industrial Property Office—was concluded in 1962 among 12 African French-speaking countries. It contains common provisions for the protection of industrial property titles and the creation of a centralised industrial property office. The Libreville Agreement was revised in 1977 and it is still in force under the title of the Bangui Agreement on the Creation of an African Intellectual Property Organization.

On the one hand, the establishment of the International Patent Institute[5] was the first result of international technical cooperation in the field of patents and offered inventors and innovators a highly valuable technical means to ascertain the degree of novelty of their inventions and to decide whether or not to continue with the procedure for granting the patent. On the other hand, the two Conventions, which were administered by the Council of Europe, set a number of basic rules which harmonised the national requirements for the filing of patent applications and have defined the minimum conditions for obtaining a valid title, thus simplifying access to patent protection. The conclusion of these international instruments may be retrospectively interpreted as a first indication of the will of European countries to lay the foundations for the building of the future European patent system.

II. The 1962 Draft Convention for a European Patent Law – The 1969 Memorandum on the Setting up of a European System for the Grant of Patents – The European Patent Convention and the Community Patent Convention

The conclusion in 1957 of the Treaty Establishing the European Economic Community (EEC) raised the question, in the framework of the common provisions regulating commerce within the territory of the Community, of the compatibility of the norms on the protection of industrial property provided for in the legislation of the Community's Member States with the Community rules on commerce. Indeed, the text of the EEC Treaty in Articles 28 and 29 prohibits the application of quantitative restrictions on imports and exports between Member States. It further specifies in Article 30 that the provisions of Articles 28 and 29 do not apply to restrictions on imports and exports justified, inter alia, by reasons of protection of industrial and commercial property. In the first instance, these provisions were interpreted in the sense that a possible conflict might have existed between one of the basic principles on which the existence of the Community itself is based—the free movement of goods and services within a single market—and the national industrial property legislation of Member States which have a national territorial scope. However, the doctrine gradually developed arguments which tended to deny possible reasons of contrast between the Community principles and the national industrial property norms of Member States, thus excluding the possibility that the latter could constitute an obstacle to the free movement of goods among EEC Member States.

[5] The International Patent Institute ceased to exist on 29 November 2000. Its competences were transferred to the European Patent Office.

The development of this line of thought laid the basis for the preparation in 1962 of the Draft Convention for a European Patent Law, which was proposed by the six EEC Member States (Belgium, the Federal Republic of Germany, France, Italy, Luxembourg and the Netherlands). This draft can be considered the first substantial proposal for the creation of an autonomous legislative system in the field of protection of inventions applicable to the entire territory of the Community. On further inspection, however, it should be noted that such a harmonisation project was, in many respects, too ambitious for the period in which it was conceived, since in the early 1960s, the European economic integration process was only taking its first steps. Indeed, the work undertaken for the preparation of the Convention was interrupted in 1964 due to the diverging positions of the participating states on the question of the scope of the text under discussion. The main point at issue was whether non-Member States of the Community could become parties to the Convention.

Between 1964 and 1968, the position of the negotiating states became more flexible and open to compromise solutions. On the one hand, such a change was largely influenced by the positive evolution of the economy of the Member States of the Community during this period and by the pressing activity of the European Free Trade Association (EFTA) in favour of a European patent system applicable not only to the Community Member States but also a larger number of European countries.[6] On the other hand, the importance of proposing at the European level a regional patent system as an alternative to the international system, which was in the process of being established at the conclusion of the negotiations for the adoption of the Patent Cooperation Treaty (PCT), whose entry into force was expected to substantially increase the number of patent applications worldwide, became apparent. The French government, under pressure from its industrial sectors, became the interpreter of all those motives and presented the EEC Council with a proposal overcoming the differences which in 1964 had caused the failure of the negotiations for the adoption of the draft Convention for a European Patent Law. Under the French proposal, the future European patent system would have consisted of two conventions.

One convention would have had an enlarged territorial basis, including non-EEC Member States. It would have provided for the grant of a European patent by a centralised European patent office by virtue of a uniform European patent legislation. After the grant, the European patent would have had the equivalent value of a national patent in each Member State.

The territorial scope of the other convention would have been limited only to the Community's Member States and would have provided for the grant of a single patent—the community patent—valid in each Member State of the Community.

[6] On the position of EFTA concerning the European patent, see EFTA Secretariat, *Building EFTA: A Free Trade in Europe (1968)*; *Eleventh Annual Report*, 1971.

The proposal was elaborated upon by a Committee of Experts, approved by the EEC Council and integrated in a Memorandum on the Setting up of a European System for the Grant of Patents of 3 March 1969.[7] The Memorandum expressly declared that in preparing a European system for the grant of patents, due account would have been taken of the Draft Convention for a European Patent Law (1962), of the Convention on the Unification of Certain Points of Substantive Law on Patents of Invention (1963) and of the draft of the PCT (1968), which was at that time still under discussion. Even though the principles contained in the Memorandum have the preliminary character of 'guidelines', they may be considered the 'birth certificate' of a complex regional legal system whose morphology has become more precise over 40 years of amendments, discussions and negotiations.

The preparatory works of the two proposed Conventions started and proceeded in parallel, leading to the adoption, respectively, in 1973 of the European Patent Convention (EPC) and in 1975 of the Community Patent Convention (CPC); this latter instrument, however, never entered into force.

The EPC was adopted in Munich on 5 October 1973 and entered into force on 7 October 1977, together with the implementing Regulations. The Convention was last substantially revised by the Act of 29 November 2000 (EPC 2000), which entered into force on 13 December 2007.

The EPC is administered by the European Patent Organization (EPO), an international organisation with its headquarters in Munich. The Convention provides for a centralised procedure for the granting of a 'European patent'. The processing of patent applications for a European patent includes an examination of the subject matter of the application, the drawing up of a search report, its publication and an opposition procedure. Such procedures are carried out by the competent divisions of the European Patent Office, which, along with the Administrative Council, constitute the principal organs of the EPO. The European patent is valid for a period of 20 years from the date of filing of the application and produces in each Member State the same effects as a national patent of that State. Once it is granted, the European patent is subject to the national patent provisions of the Member State in which it is granted. In summary, the EPC has established a regional patent system centralising the procedure for the granting of a patent, leaving to each Member State the competence, under national law, for the maintenance of the granted patent and for the enforcement of the exclusive rights by the owner of the patent.[8]

The EPC 2000 constitutes the first substantial revision of the 1973 text of the Convention. It takes into account international instruments in force, such as the Agreement on Trade-Related Aspects of Intellectual Property Rights (hereinafter

[7] For the text of the Memorandum, see *International Review of Industrial Property and Copyright Law*-IIC, 1970, 26.

[8] On the EPC, see R Singer, *The European Patent Convention* (revised English edn by R Lunzer, London, Sweet & Maxwell, 1995); H Hullrich, 'Patent Protection in Europe: Integrating Europe into the Community or the Community into Europe?' (2002) 8(4) *European Law Journal* 433.

the TRIPS Agreement) (1994) and the Patent Law Treaty (PLT) (2000), and introduces procedures with a view to simplifying the filing of European patent applications, their examination and the granting of European patents. The revised text of the Convention applies to European patent applications filed and European patents granted after the entry into force of the Revising Act.

The preparatory work for the other Convention proposed in the 1969 Memorandum was concluded in Luxembourg with adoption on 1 December 1975 of the Community Patent Convention (CPC) and of the relevant implementing Regulations. The aim of the Convention was not to duplicate, even in part, the provisions of the EPC, but to extend in a unitary manner in the Member States of the Community the effects of the European patent granted under the procedures of the EPC. The CPC opened the way for the granting of a supranational property title for the protection of inventions (the 'Community patent'), which had a unitary and autonomous character and was valid across the entire territory of the Community, without interfering with the right of each Member State to retain its national patent system. From this perspective, the EPO had the task of administering the procedure for the granting of the Community patent. Such task was carried out through ad hoc created organs: an Administrative Division, a Revocation Division and an Appeal Division. In view of the CPC's declared intention of pursuing the aims of the EEC Treaty, jurisdiction for the interpretation and application of the Convention was entrusted to the Community's High Court of Justice.

The 1975 text of the CPC was not ratified. One of the main reasons for the lack of ratification was the adoption in 1970 of the PCT and in 1973 of the EPC, two international instruments which substantially modified the structure of the international system for the protection of inventions and demanded considerable efforts on the part of the patent offices of the Member States in preparing the relevant ratifications of the newly adopted instruments.

In 1989 there was a late attempt to give new vitality to the Convention. On 15 December 1989, a revised text of the CPC—called the Agreement on the Community Patent—was finalised. However, this text did not receive the number of ratifications required for its entry into force.[9]

The non-entry into force of the CPC meant that the EPC, which was originally devised to interact with the CPC in the establishment of an integrated European patent system, remained the only instrument to provide the mechanism for the protection of inventions at a European level. The subsequent history of the functioning of this Convention proves that it was not only a major factor in the harmonisation of national patent laws of Member States, but that today is at the centre of the new process for the creation of a unitary integrated system for the protection of inventive activity in Europe.

[9] On the CPC, see F Savignon, *Convention de Luxembourg du 15 décembre 1975—Le brevet communautaire*, La Propriété industrielle, février 1976; Hullrich (n 8).

The failure of the CPC to enter into force was not only due, as already noted, to the legislative and administrative efforts connected with the entry into force of the EPC and the PCT, but also to a number of intrinsic reasons, such as the high costs envisaged for the maintenance of the Community patent (in particular those relating to the translation of patent documents into the various languages of the Community) and to the complex jurisdictional system proposed. It is also interesting to note that the difficulties existing in 1989 anticipated those which in future decades will characterise the negotiations for the adoption of the Regulation on the community patent. From this perspective, the preparatory work for the adoption of the CPC and the reasons which determined the failure of its entry into force represent a meaningful precedent in the framework of the evolution of the idea of creating a Community patent. To fully appreciate this evolution, it must be placed in the context of the substantive changes undergone by the international system for the protection of intellectual property during the last two decades of the twentieth century in relation to the significant transformation of the global economy.

III. Parallel International Developments: The PCT

While the work for the adoption of the EPC and the CPC was progressing, another international instrument—the PCT—was prepared, negotiated and adopted under the auspices of the WIPO. Following a proposal by the US government in 1966, the drafting of the PCT was completed relatively quickly in 1969. The treaty was signed in Washington DC on 9 June 1970 and entered into force on 1 June 1978. It is administered by the WIPO.[10]

The PCT deals with the question of the duplication of administrative acts when protection for an invention is sought in more than one country at the same time. It follows the general pattern of other international registration agreements[11] and has established a complex and composite mechanism for the rationalisation of the procedures for the filing of patent applications, their examination and the diffusion of the technical information contained therein, which has been very well received by the users of the patent system.[12]

The PCT has two main objectives. On the one hand, it offers applicants a unitary and simplified way to request the protection of their inventions in several countries at the same time and, with the 'international search report', it supplies the elements necessary to decide whether to pursue the request of protection or to abandon it. On the other hand, it reduces the burden on national industrial

[10] On the drafting and adoption of the PCT, see *Principal Documents of the Washington Diplomatic Conference on the Patent Cooperation Treaty* (Geneva, BIRPI, 1970).

[11] See n 1 above.

[12] For statistical information on the international applications under the PCT, see *WIPO-PCT International Patent System-Yearly Review. Developments and Performance*, WIPO, Geneva.

property offices in relation to administering patent applications, concentrating in the International Bureau of the WIPO the main procedures relating to the filing of patent applications, such as the examination of formal requirements and the examination of novelty requirements, the latter of which has not been always provided for in the national legislation of certain states.[13]

The procedure under the PCT provides for two phases: the so-called 'international phase', relating to the filing of the international patent application, the international search, the international publication, the international preliminary examination, and the so-called 'national phase', during which the application is dealt with by the national office of each designated state in which protection is sought, according to national law. While the procedure provided for by the EPC leads to the granting of a unitary industrial property title, the European patent, the procedure under the PCT simplifies the procedures for the filing of the international patent application, leaving the grant or the refusal of the patent to the national office of each designated state.

The fact that the preparation and the adoption of the EPC and the PCT took place roughly during the same period (1966–78) proves that states and interested industrial groups, both at the European and the international level, were finally inclined to put aside their traditional hesitations and adopt a multilateral system of protection of inventions which could offer inventors two complementary routes—one regional and one international—for the protection of the results of their inventive activity. As an additional proof of this determination and in order to maximise the result of the procedures of the two instruments, these have been programmed to interact. Part X of the EPC (Articles 150–58) contains provisions establishing a link with the PCT, thus offering the possibility of obtaining a European patent based on an international application under the PCT. Furthermore, the interaction between the two treaties has been strengthened by the conclusion of a specific cooperation agreement of 7 October 1978 between the EPO and the WIPO.

IV. 1978–94: Towards a Global Protection of Intellectual Property Rights. The Project for the Revision of the Paris Convention for the Protection of Industrial Property and the TRIPS Agreement

The entry into force of the EPC and the PCT in 1977 and 1978, respectively, marked the beginning of a deep change which in subsequent years influenced

[13] On the PCT, see the abundant information material prepared by the WIPO (www.wipo.int/en/registration/pct).

the entire structure of the international protection of industrial property. This change, however, should not be considered as an isolated event typically related to the industrial property field, but should also be understood as an integral part of the change in the global economic parameters to which the General Agreement on Tariffs and Trade (GATT) largely contributed and which, under the name 'globalisation', would dominate every aspect of human activity, public and private.

The gradual reduction of customs duties immediately after the end of the Second World War by the countries adhering to the GATT and continued systematically with a succession of periodical multilateral negotiations[14]—the so-called 'Rounds'—yielded the result of stimulating the flow of international commerce and developed an increased interdependence between the commercial systems of the majority of countries. In this context, the spreading phenomenon of counterfeiting was rightly perceived as a substantial impediment to the establishment of free commerce worldwide. The attention of the international community was drawn to this phenomenon in the framework of the negotiations in 1978 of the Tokyo Round,[15] although no contrasting measures were adopted on that occasion.[16] It should be noted, nevertheless, that for the first time a specific situation, inherent to the protection of intellectual property, became a substantive element in the discussions on the establishment of new rules governing international trade.[17] To confront a situation which was widespread and was becoming an alarming form of piracy, with negative repercussions on commercial exchanges and on the interests of consumers, two alternative approaches appeared possible: the existing international norms on counterfeiting would have to be changed or new norms would have to be created. Within the GATT system, there was a non-homogeneous group of norms on patents, trademarks, copyright and misleading practices, while the international instruments administered by the WIPO did not contain provisions directed towards the protection of intellectual property rights before national jurisdictions and relating to the settlement of disputes among Member States. In the face of this situation, two tendencies were developed. On the one hand, between 1974 and 1984, the WIPO had begun preparatory working in view of a revision of the Paris Convention. The aim of the proposed revision, which was to follow the last administrative revision in Stockholm in 1967, was intended to introduce substantive changes to the Convention provisions,

[14] After the conclusion of the GATT of 30 October 1947, the following GATT 'rounds' took place: Geneva, 1947; Annecy (France), 1949; Torquay (England), 1951; Geneva, 1964–67 (the 'Kennedy Round'); Geneva, 1973–79 (the 'Tokyo Round'); Geneva, 1986–94 (the 'Uruguay Round'). The WTO was established following the conclusion of the Uruguay Round. At present, the 'Doha Development Round', which started in 2001, is still in progress.

[15] See the intervention of R Yerxa, Vice Director General of the WTO, at the Third Global Congress on Combating Counterfeiting and Piracy, Geneva, 30–31 January 2007.

[16] However, mention should be made of the Anti-Counterfeiting Trade Act (ACTA), which was negotiated between 2006 and 2010. It was signed on 1 October 2011 by eight states and on 26 January 2012 by 22 states. It was never ratified and is the subject of severe criticisms.

[17] See the Agreement on Measures to Discourage the Importation of Counterfeited Goods, GATT Doc L/5382 (18 October 1982).

in particular in the field of patents, in order to take into account the requests of developing countries for the establishment of a special regime applicable to those countries. On the other hand, during the preparatory phase of the Uruguay Round, which started officially with the Ministerial Conference at Punta del Este in September 1978, new proposed norms were elaborated, which aimed at reducing and limiting the distortions and obstacles caused to international commerce by the inadequate protection of intellectual property rights and proposing the setting up of multilateral principles, sanctions and rules against international counterfeiting. Even if clearly in contrast, the two alternatives evolved in parallel. While the developing countries privileged WIPO efforts for a revision of the Paris Convention, the industrialised countries, even those negotiating within the WIPO for a revision of the Convention, were openly in favour of a system encompassing the principles of protection of intellectual property administered by the GATT, accompanied by the mechanism of sanctions. For the sake of completeness, it should be recalled that a number of intergovernmental organisations, such as the Organisation for Economic Co-operation and Development (OECD), the United Nations Conference on Trade and Development (UNCTAD) and the United Nations Organization (UN), participated in the debate with studies and proposals.

The attempt, which was to a large extent anachronistic, carried on under the auspices of the WIPO to revise the Paris Convention failed after the Revision Conference met four times without success in 1980, 1981, 1982 and 1984.[18] The failure to revise the Convention proved, on the one hand, that amendments to the international system of industrial property protection should take place with the adoption of new norms and not with the revision of existing ones and, on the other hand, favoured the adding to the agenda of the Uruguay Round the question of 'trade-related aspects of intellectual property rights'. From a more general point of view, this also meant the end of an approach to the international protection of intellectual property, typical of the nineteenth century, based on a system of 'unions' among states, in which no sanction was forseen.

The Uruguay Round started in 1986 and completed its work in Marrakesh in 1994. After eight years of complex negotiations, the Round adopted the Agreement Establishing the World Trade Organization (WTO). Appendix 1C, an integral part of the WTO Agreement, contains the TRIPS Agreement.[19] The result of this important normative effort is a set of norms, which for the first time in the history of the international protection of intellectual property encompass in a single instrument the newly revised substantive provisions of the main treaties

[18] See A Bogsch, *Brief History of the First 25 Years of the World Intellectual Property Organization* (Geneva, WIPO, 1992).

[19] On the TRIPS Agreement, see D Gervais, *The TRIPS Agreement: Drafting History and Analysis* (London, Sweet & Maxwell, 1998); T Cottier, *The Agreement on Trade Related Aspects of Intellectual Property Rights* (New York, Springer, 2005).

and conventions in the field.[20] These treaty provisions include, on the one hand, a mechanism of sanctions in order to guarantee their enforcement and, on the other hand, adopt the principles governing the economic relations between states in the framework of the WTO Agreement. A further result of the TRIPS Agreement is the harmonisation without precedent of the intellectual property legislation of the Member States.

During the Round, the position of developing countries, which were originally critical of the establishment of an agreement within the GATT, gradually changed. The system of protection of intellectual property rights proposed by the TRIPS Agreement was perceived as a tool which would have facilitated the transfer of technology from industrialised to developing countries and would have contributed to the development of local technologies.[21]

The evolution of the regional and international systems of industrial property protection described above, in particular those relating to patents, contains in itself the elements which have contributed to a large extent to the relaunching on a new basis of the project for the adoption of a Community patent, which was abandoned a decade earlier, following the non-entry into force of the CPC.

V. New Attempts at the Establishment of the Community Patent System

The adoption of the TRIPS Agreement brought an ample understanding of the importance of the role of the patent system, in general, as an instrument of economic policy and, in particular, concerning its function in international trade, as a basic element in the transfer of technology. Such awareness motivated on the part of industry a request for more specific options for the protection of innovation which would take into account new development and marketing strategies.

Indeed, following the adoption of the TRIPS Agreement and notwithstanding the leading role played by the EPC in harmonising national patent laws and in offering a simplified and efficient procedure for the protection of inventions in several European countries, the idea of establishing a unitary patent system in the Member States of the EC began to be debated once again. In 1997, this new tendency was summarised in the Green Paper on the Community Patent and the

[20] Article 3(1) of the TRIPS Agreement refers expressly to the following intellectual property conventions and treaties: the Paris Convention for the Protection of Industrial Property (1883); the Berne Convention for the Protection of Literary and Artistic Works (1886); the International Convention for the Protection of Performers, Producers of Phonograms and Broadcasting Organizations (1961); and the Treaty on Intellectual Property in Respect of Integrated Circuits (1989).

[21] See Gervais (n 19).

Patent System in Europe,[22] presented by the Commission, followed in 1998 by a series of consultations, culminating on 5 February 1999 with the adoption by the Commission of a Communication containing the main elements of the future Community patent system.[23] On 24 March 2000, the EC Council, meeting in Lisbon, approved the idea of creating a Community patent, underlying its importance in reaching the objectives of the Community.

[22] Commission, 'Promoting Innovation Through Patents. Green Paper on the Community Patent and the Patent System in Europe' COM (1997) 314 final.

[23] Commission, 'Promoting Innovation through Patents. The Follow-up to the Green Paper on the Community Patent and the Patent System in Europe' COM (1999) 42 final.

3

The First Phase of the Negotiations for the Adoption of a Regulation on the Community Patent

I. The Commission Proposal for a Council Regulation on the Community Patent (2000)

The decision taken by the EC Council at the Lisbon meeting on 24 March 2000 was followed on 1 August of the same year by a Commission proposal for a Council Regulation on the Community Patent.[1] As in the case of the Regulation on the Community Trade Mark and of the Regulation on the Community Design,[2] the main legal basis of the Commission proposal was Article 308[3] of the Treaty Establishing the European Community (TEC). The Regulation was the legal instrument chosen for completing the structure of the industrial property Community system. This was an ad hoc choice made to underline the need to guarantee the principle of unitary effect of the Community patent across the entire territory of the Community. The focal point of the proposal was the creation of a link between the future Community patent system and that administered by the EPO, by way of the Community, as such, adhering to the EPC. By virtue of such adhesion, a European patent application filed according to the EPC could designate the territory of the Community and ask for the grant of a Community patent by the EPO.

The declared purpose of the Commission proposal was the establishment of a supranational patent right having a unitary character and applicable within the

[1] Commission, 'Proposal for a Council Regulation on the Community patent' COM (2000) 412 final. In this document, see the Introductory Memorandum containing information on the Commission proposal and a detailed commentary on the individual articles.

[2] Regulation (CE) 40/94 of 22 December 1994 and Regulation (CE) 6/2002 of 12 December 2001.

[3] This article refers to the so-called 'theory of implicit powers', originally elaborated upon by the US Supreme Court and adopted by the European Court of Justice. It implies that when an action of the Community is deemed necessary in order to reach a Community objective, even if the relevant powers to this effect are not provided for in the Treaty, the Council may, subject to a consultation procedure, take the necessary implementing measures. On this question, see P Eeckhout, *EU External Relations Law* (Oxford, Oxford University Press, 2011).

territory of the Community. The unitary character of such a right was essential to overcome any possible distortion caused to competition from the territorial scope of national patent rights, with the aim of maintaining the free movement of patented products within the Community. Therefore, the Community patent should coexist, on the one hand, with national patents and, on the other hand, with European patents so as to offer inventors and innovators three alternatives when protecting the results of their inventive activity in Europe: the national patent, the European patent and the Community patent.

The Commission proposal for a Council Regulation on the Community patent deserves due attention and a detailed examination. Indeed, even if in the course of a decade it has undergone several substantial modifications, it nevertheless constitutes the platform on which the negotiations for the building up of the Community patent system were based and to some extent it anticipates the difficulties which were actually encountered. It comprises a 'Preamble' and six chapters:

- Chapter I—General Provisions;
- Chapter II—Patent Law;
- Chapter III—Renewal, Lapse and Invalidity of the Community Patent;
- Chapter IV—Jurisdiction and Procedure in Legal Actions Relating to the Community Patent;
- Chapter V—Impact of National Law;
- Chapter VI—Final Provisions.

In the 'Preamble', three main questions are considered. First, there is the relationship between the future Community patent system and the European patent system, and the function of this relationship in the structure of the Community system for the protection of inventions. This is a focal point in the creation of the Community patent system as it implies an ad hoc modification of the EPC implementing Regulations in order to render the two instruments compatible and to allow the European Patent Office to perform its new functions of examining and granting the Community patent. Second, in order to avoid the monopoly created by the Community patent constituting an impediment to the free exchange of products in the internal market, a system of compulsory licences should be established and the Commission should be given decision-making powers over the matter. Commission decisions should be subject to appeal before the Court of First Instance and the Court of Justice of the European Union. In the third instance, for reasons of legal certainty, one court—the Community Intellectual Property Court—should have jurisdiction over all actions relating to the Community patent, in particular those relating to infringement and validity.

Chapter I, 'General Provisions', establishes the category of the Community patent law that applies to the patents granted as Community patents by the European Patent Office. This is autonomous legislation which coexists with the national patent laws and the European patent system under the EPC. The Community patent has a unitary character in the sense that it is issued, transferred, declared invalid or can expire only with respect of the territory of the whole Community. It has an autonomous character in the sense that it is subject to the provisions of the Regulation and to the principles of Community law. 'Application for a Community patent' means an application for a European patent designating the territory of the Community.

Chapter II, 'Patent Law', contains three groups of substantive law provisions. The first group is the norms governing the acquisition of the right to the Community patent, including the relationship between employees and employers, the scope of the rights conferred and the change of ownership. The second group is the provisions relating to the effects of the Community patent and the Community patent application, such as the prohibition of direct and indirect use of the invention, the limitation of the effects and the exhaustion of rights conferred by the Community patent, the rights conferred by the Community patent application after publication and the burden of proof in the case of a process patent for a new product. The third group is the rules concerning the Community patent as an object of property, such as the transfer of the patent and the conditions applicable to the licence of right and the compulsory licence. As regards this group of norms, it should be noted that they reflect, to a large extent, the corresponding provisions of the CPC, the EPC, the Paris Convention and the TRIPS Agreement.

Chapter III, 'Renewal, Lapse and Invalidity of the Community Patent', regulates the life of the Community patent. On the one hand, it deals with the procedures for the renewal and lapse of the patent and, on the other hand, the grounds for invalidity and the effects of invalidity of the patent.

Chapter IV, 'Jurisdiction and Procedure in Legal Actions Relating to the Community Patent', covers three procedural aspects where the Community patent is subject to legal action. First, the Community Intellectual Property Court has exclusive jurisdiction for actions concerning the validity, infringement and use of the Community patent. An appeal may be lodged against the decisions of the Court with its Chamber of Appeals. Second, national courts of Member States have jurisdiction over actions which do not fall within the jurisdiction of the Court, such as proceedings relating to the right of the patent between employers and employees. Unless otherwise specified, the Brussels Convention on Jurisdiction and the Enforcement of Judgments in Civil and Commercial Matters applies to such actions and to the relevant decisions. In the third instance, national arbitration rules apply to arbitration proceedings, with the proviso that they cannot invalidate the Community patent.

Chapter V, 'Impact of National Law', sets out the principle of the prohibition of simultaneous protection for the same invention granted to the same inventor by a national patent and a Community patent. The same applies to national utility models and utility certificates, where such titles are provided for in the national law of the Member State.

Chapter VI, 'Final Provisions', contains norms for the establishment of a Register of Community Patents, for the publication of the *Community Patent*

Bulletin, including entries made in the Register, and sets out the procedure for the preparation of the implementing Regulations and the rules relating to annual and renewal fees.

II. The Common Political Approach (2003)

Following its presentation in August 2000, the Commission proposal on the Community patent was the subject of extensive debates which generated a considerable number of documents containing comments on and amendments to the original text.[4] It soon became evident that the main questions on which it was necessary to reach a compromise were those concerning the structure of the future jurisdictional system, the language regime applicable to the Community patent applications and patents, the costs, the role of the national offices of the Member States in administering the Community patent and the distribution of the renewal fees for the Community patent between the EPO, and the national offices according to a distribution key to be decided by the Council.

With the aim of conciliating diverging positions and facilitating the reaching of an agreement, on 3 March 2003 the Council adopted the text of a document entitled 'Common Political Approach', proposing a possible compromise solution on each question under discussion:

- 'Jurisdictional System'. This would consist of a unitary court—the Court for the Community Patent—having exclusive competence in proceedings concerning Community patents. Appeals against final decisions of the Court would be brought before the Court of First Instance. It was foreseen that the Court would be established by 2010.
- 'Language Regime'. Up until the grant of the Community patent, the trilingual regime (English, French and German) provided for under the EPC was applicable. The application would be filed in one of the three languages of the EPC, accompanied, at the time of the grant, by a translation of the claims into the other two EPC languages. Where the application was filed in a non-EPC language and accompanied by a translation into one of the EPC languages,

[4] See, in particular, Opinion of the Economic and Social Council on the Proposal for a Council regulation on the Community Patent (SEC/2001/411); Commission Staff Working Paper: A Community Policy for the Realization of a Community Patent in the Context of a Revision of the European Patent Convention (SEC/2001/744 final); Commission Working Document on the Planned Community Patent Jurisdiction (Commission, 'Commission working document on the planned community patent jurisdiction' COM (2002) 480 final). See also the following revised texts of the Commission's proposal: the Presidency-document 8539/03; the Presidency-document 10404/03 (PI 53); the Secretariat of the Council-document 10728/03; the Secretariat of the Council-document 15086/03.

the translation costs would be borne by a common system. Following the grant, the claims would be translated into all official Community languages.[5]

— 'Costs'. The renewal fees for a Community patent should not exceed the corresponding renewal fees for an average European patent.
— 'Role of National Offices'. The EPO would play a central role in the administration of the Community patent and would be responsible for the examination of applications and the granting of the relevant patent. The relationship between the EPO and national offices of Member States would be regulated by ad hoc agreements specifying the details of the reciprocal cooperation.
— 'Distribution of Fees'. Renewal fees would be shared between the EPO and the national offices: 50 per cent would be kept by the EPO to cover its costs, while the remaining 50 per cent would be distributed among national offices, according to a distribution scheme to be established by the Council.

Notwithstanding the 'Common Political Approach' that was formally adopted in March 2003,[6] during the subsequent meetings of 28 November 2003 and 12 March 2004, the Council had no choice but to admit the impossibility of reaching a political compromise on the basis of this text. In particular, on the question of the language regime, the document was rejected, mainly because of the strong opposition of future users of the system.

III. Commission Proposals on Jurisdictional Matters (2003)

A few months after the publication of the Common Political Approach, the Commission presented two documents on jurisdictional matters, a necessary complement to the Community patent system: 'Proposal for a Council Decision Conferring Jurisdiction on the Court of Justice in Disputes Relating to the Community Patent'[7] and 'Proposal for a Council Decision Establishing the Community Patent Court and Concerning Appeals Before the Court of First Instance'.[8]

The purpose of these proposals was, first, to remove from the Common Political Approach, which was rejected as a whole, the questions relating to

[5] See the Agreement on the Application of Article 65 of the Convention for the Grant of European Patents (London Agreement) of 17 October 2000, which entered into force on 1 May 2008. The purpose of the Agreement is to reduce the translation costs of European patents granted under the EPC. The system provided for in the London Agreement has been taken into account in the elaboration of the 'Common Political Approach' and will continue to be referred to in the course of the negotiations on the language regime.

[6] Council Document 7159/03 of 7 March 2003.

[7] Commission, 'Proposal for a Council Decision conferring jurisdiction on the Court of Justice in disputes relating to the Community patent' COM (2003) 827 final.

[8] Commission, 'Proposal for a Council Decision establishing the Community Patent Court and concerning appeals before the Court of First Instance' COM (2003) 828 final.

jurisdiction and make them a separate point of discussion. In addition, the proposals aimed to clarify its components in view of their impact in the legal systems of the Member States, it being understood that their final objective was to confirm the principle that patent protection of inventions within the Community had to be based on a unitary jurisdiction and uniform rules.

The legal basis for the establishment of the Community patent jurisdictional system proposed by the Commission is constituted by Articles 229a and 225a, which were introduced into the EC Treaty by Article 2 of the Treaty of Nice, which entered into force on 1 February 2003.

First, it was proposed that the jurisdictional responsibilities of the Court of Justice should include questions relating to the Community patent, so that the Court could be declared competent in the matter. This was the subject of the first proposal made by the Commission, based on Article 229a. This provision authorises the Council to adopt norms declaring the Court of Justice competent in controversies involving Community industrial property titles in general and, specifically, Community patents. According to this proposal, the Court of Justice should be competent for a number of actions relating to the Community patent, such as infringement and validity; actions concerning the use of the invention after the publication of the Community patent application and the right based on prior use of the invention; provisional protection measures; damages and compensation measures; and penalty payments in case of non-compliance with the Community Court decision to act or to abstain from an act.

Second, a proposal was made for the creation of a judicial panel within the framework of the Court of Justice—the Community Patent Court—that was competent to exercise at first instance the jurisdiction in disputes relating to the Community patent. This was the subject of the second proposal made by the Commission, based on Articles 225a and 220, as far as appeals were concerned. According to this proposal, the jurisdiction of the Community Patent Court should be centralised and specialised, in line with the unitary character of the Community patent. The Court should be composed of seven judges, including the President, assisted by technical experts. The procedure should be carried out in each language of the Community and its choice made dependent on the domicile of the defendant. A Patent Appeal Chamber should be set up within the Court of First Instance according to Article 220 and should be competent to hear and determine appeals against decisions of the Community Patent Court under Article 225. In principle, Community patent disputes should be heard by the Court of First Instance as a second and last resort. A further appeal to the Court of Justice was not foreseen.

These proposals did not meet with the approval of the Member States. Some expressed themselves in favour of the model offered by the draft European Patent Litigation Agreement (EPLA),[9] while others supported the idea of a specific

[9] The first EPLA proposal was made in 1966 as a Protocol to the EPC. It envisages the creation of an integrated jurisdictional system for European patent disputes.

Community jurisdiction, based on the EC Treaty, in disputes relating to European and Community patents.

IV. The 2006 Consultation and the Subsequent Commission Communication on the Strengthening of the Patent System in Europe (2007)

At the end of 2003, notwithstanding the Commission's efforts, there was a risk that the negotiations would fail and not continue. There was general disagreement over the main questions under discussion, in particular those relating to the language regime to be adopted and to jurisdictional matters. These two subjects, because of their direct influence on the administrative and jurisdictional systems of Member States, would continue to constitute elements of disagreement in the course of the future negotiations. With the view to providing new momentum to the debate, in March 2004 the Commission prepared a revised version of its 2000 proposal for a Council Regulation on the Community patent, which, however, did not produce the expected result.[10] The revised text included, on the one hand, the solutions proposed in the Common Political Approach and, on the other hand, the Commission proposals on jurisdictional matters.[11]

Notwithstanding this situation, the Commission continued to support the ideas expressed in its 2000 proposal[12] on the need to adopt, in the context of an increasingly competitive global economy, an affordable Community patent system which should become an incentive for innovation, competition and economic growth. According to this line of thought, the Commission opted to act in two converging directions with a view to offering to negotiators as many elements of evaluation as possible. On the one hand, it promoted an analytical study of 27 industrial sectors to highlight the features which should make up the framework of the Community industrial policy. The results of this study were included in a Commission communication of 5 October 2005. On the other hand, on 16 January 2006 it launched a consultation with a view to discovering the opinions of the users on the patent system in Europe. To this end, it asked which changes would be most appropriate to improve the development of innovation, competition, employment and economic growth. The consultation was based on a Commission questionnaire of 9 January 2006 and the deadline for submitting replies expired on 12 April 2006. It obtained the impressive number of 2,515

[10] Council Document 7119/04 of 8 March 2004.

[11] See sections II and III of this chapter.

[12] Commission, 'Proposal for a Council Regulation on the Community patent' COM (2000) 214 final.

replies. On 12 July 2006, the Commission organised a public hearing in Brussels to discuss, on the basis of an ad hoc report, the results of the consultation. The questionnaire was structured into four parts:[13]

— 'Basic Principles and Features of the Patent System'. The majority of answers insisted on the need to develop a comprehensive innovation policy in Europe to respond to challenges from major non-European countries (for example, the US and Japan) and emerging economic powers such as China and India, and pointed out the importance of rendering the patent an incontestable title through a quality control system in examination and prior art search.
— 'Community Patent as a Priority for the EU'. The majority favoured the creation of the Community patent as means to ameliorate the current situation in Europe regarding the protection of inventions. However, the Common Political Approach was in general rejected on the grounds of an unsatisfactory language regime and inadequate proposed jurisdictional arrangements. The Commission was requested to further elaborate on those two elements.
— 'The European Patent System and the European Patent Litigation Agreement (EPLA)'. On the question of jurisdiction, the majority of answers favoured substantial changes in the current litigation regime which would render the procedures simple, rapid, transparent and economic within the framework of a good level of centralisation. Furthermore, general support was expressed for Community involvement in the EPLA in consideration of its practical and pragmatic approach and creating the right balance between simple access to courts and legal certainty through centralisation.
— 'Approximation and Mutual Recognition of National Patents'. On the one hand, the importance of the substantive harmonisation of patent law achieved by the EPC and the TRIPS Agreement was singled out, while, on the other hand, the idea of mutual recognition of national patents was widely rejected as not feasible due to the significant differences in experience and expertise which still existed among national patent offices.[14]

In line with the opinions expressed by the majority of the replies received to the questionnaire and aware of the importance of speeding up of the resumption of negotiations, on 29 March 2007 the Commission published a communication to the European Parliament and the Council entitled 'Enhancing the Patent System

[13] For an economic opinion on the questionnaire, see F Lévêque and Y Ménière, 'Academic Response to the European Commission's Questionnaire on the Patent System in Europe: An Academic Approach' (2008) 28 *World Patent Information* 305.

[14] In his intervention of 29 March 2007, the European Commissioner Charlie McCreevy summarised the position of the Community's authorities on the results of the Consultation as follows: 'There was strong support for a cost-effective Community patent, including sound litigation arrangements, while at the same time improving the current patent system in Europe. In October 2006 the European Parliament supported this line and urged us to explore all possible ways of improving the patent granting and litigation systems in the European Union. This calls for a combined effort by Member States and the Community institutions.'

in Europe'.[15] This document is one of the first examples of intervention by the Commission, which would be frequently adopted in the coming years, aimed at presenting specific compromise solutions in order to stimulate the debate on critical issues under discussion.

After having noted that the present European patent system was more expensive than that of the US and Japan, and that national patent litigation systems in the EU were unreasonably costly and led to multiple forms of litigation on the same patent issue in several Member States, the Commission considered two main issues under discussion: the Community patent and the jurisdictional system. On the question of the Community patent, the document reaffirmed the Commission's opinion that the Community patent remained the key tool for the challenges with which Europe was confronted in the field of patents and innovation, and the most affordable and legally secure solution. In this context, the criticism formulated on the Common Political Approach appeared justified and needed to be taken into account. With respect to the language regime, the Commission expressed the opinion that, in particular for small and medium-sized enterprises (SMEs), it should be possible to find effective solutions, to be explored with Member States, to improve the language regime with a view to reducing translation costs while increasing legal certainty. On the question of jurisdiction, the Commission believed that consensus could be built on the basis of an integrated approach which should combine features of both the EPLA and a specific Community jurisdiction.

In order to promote a rapid follow up to the Commission's proposals, on 12 July 2007 a document entitled 'Towards an Enhanced Patent Litigation System and a Community Patent—How to Take Discussions Further' was published by the Council.[16]

[15] Commission, 'Enhancing the patent system in Europe' COM (2007) 29 March 2007.

[16] Council Document 11622/07 of 12 July 2007.

4

The Second Phase of the Negotiations for the Adoption of a Regulation on the Community Patent: Enhanced Cooperation

I. Stagnation of the Negotiations: General Considerations 2008–11

At the beginning of 2008, it was evident that in the absence of a fast, coherent and unitary response on the part of the Member States to the numerous questions which emerged from the 2006 Consultation, the negotiations for the adoption of a Council Regulation on the Community patent had reached the point of no return. It was also evident that because of the rigid positions often adopted by certain delegations, which reflected a similarly rigid vision of the respective national administrations, the long-awaited answers could have not been given in a relative short timeframe. However, notwithstanding an unfavourable climate for a resumption of the debates and negotiations, the Commission and the Presidencies actively worked to present solutions which could bring about a consensus. The period of 2008–11 was characterised, on the one hand, by a series of proposals relating to the Community patent in an attempt to explore compromise solutions, in particular on the complex question of the language regime and, on the other hand, by the debate on the creation of a unitary jurisdictional system on patent disputes, which could be compatible with the EC Treaties.

II. The Decision Authorising the 'Enhanced Cooperation' in the Area of the Creation of Unitary Patent Protection (2010)

On the questions related to the Community patent, the Slovenian Presidency presented during the first half of 2008 two combined proposals[1] offering, on the one

[1] Council Document 6985/08 of 28 February 2008 and Council Document 8928/08 of 28 April 2008.

hand, an alternative translation system for the claims in patent applications and, on the other hand, a mechanism for the distribution of patent levies. As to the translation system for claims, according to the first alternative, the patent owner could have chosen the language in which the claims would have been translated; in such a case, however, the legal effect of the patent would have been limited to the Member States into whose languages it had been translated. The second alternative proposed the creation of a centralised translation service, providing automated translations. Concerning the distribution of patent levies, it was proposed that 50 per cent of such fees would go to the EPO and the remaining 50 per cent would go to the national offices of Member States according to a distribution key yet to be determined. These proposals constituted a 'package' whose components were discussed during 2008 and 2009 without any significant result being achieved. It should be noted, however, that the elements of the package anticipate those on which a final agreement would be reached in the following years.

In the second half of 2010, the Commission, supported by the Belgian Presidency and by the Council, presented a series of proposals[2] reaffirming, in essence, the idea that the language regime of the Council Regulation on the Translation Arrangements for the EU Patents should be built on the well-functioning trilingual system of the EPO. These attempts did not meet with the approval of a number of increasingly intransigent delegations so that, at the extraordinary Council meeting of 10 November 2010, despite all the efforts and concessions made, a number of Member States would not accept the proposed final compromise and thus unanimity could not be reached. This situation was further confirmed on 10 December 2010.

In the framework of these events, it should be recalled that on 1 December 2009, the Treaty of Lisbon of 13 December 2007 entered into force. This Treaty modifies the Treaty on European Union (TEU) and the EEC Treaty, which became the Treaty on the Functioning of the European Union (TFEU). In this context, the term 'Community' is substituted by 'European Union'. This instrument has operated an important reform of the legal and administrative structure of the EU, introducing changes with a view to ameliorating the functioning of the European institutions and the decision-making process, remodelling the internal and external policies and the legislative system.

The entry into force of the Lisbon Treaty placed the whole project for the adoption of a Regulation on the Community patent in a new perspective.[3] In this context, of particular relevance are the provisions of Article 118 TFEU. Pursuant to Article 118(1), a patent as European intellectual property title, with validity on the entire territory of the EU, may be established under the ordinary legislative

[2] Commission, 'Proposal for a Council Regulation (EU) on the translation arrangements for the European Union patent' COM (2010) 350, Council Document 14377/10 of 6 October 2010 and Council Document 15395/10 of 9 November 2010.

[3] See Council Document 16113/09 of 27 November 2009 and Council Document 17229/09 of 7 December 2009.

procedure, while under Article 118(2), a special legislative procedure requires unanimity in the Council for the establishment of the language arrangements of these titles. The fact that at the Council meeting of 10 November 2010, it was recorded—and was later confirmed on 10 December 2010—that no unanimity was reached on the proposed translation arrangements should be understood in the light of the provisions of Article 118.

The negative outcome of the negotiations had to some extent been foreseen. Indeed, during the Council meeting of 11 October 2010, several Member States were concerned that the objectives of the proposal for a Council Regulation on a unitary patent could not be attained within a reasonable period of time. They indicated that they were prepared to consider the possibility of establishing such a system within the framework of 'enhanced cooperation' according to the provisions of Article 20 TEU. This intention was confirmed at the Council meeting of 25 November 2010. Under the circumstances, 12 Member States (Denmark, Estonia, Finland, France, Germany, Lithuania, Luxembourg, the Netherlands, Poland, Slovenia, Sweden and the UK) formally asked the Commission to submit to the Council a proposal for the establishment of enhanced cooperation in the field of unitary patent protection. The proposal was formulated by the Commission to the Council on 14 December 2010.[4] In the meantime, 13 additional Member States (Austria, Belgium, Bulgaria, Cyprus, the Czech Republic, Greece, Hungary, Ireland, Latvia, Malta, Portugal, Romania and Slovakia) joined the first 12 Member States, giving a total of 25 Member States. The Commission's proposal was adopted by the Council on 10 March 2011,[5] which thus authorised the enhanced cooperation. Italy and Spain communicated their intention not to participate in the cooperation.[6]

III. The Legal Basis of 'Enhanced Cooperation': The Council Decision of 11 March 2011

It should noted first of all that measures relating to the establishment of 'enhanced cooperation' were introduced into the EU legal system by Article 20 TEU and are further regulated by Title III (Articles 326–34) of the TFEU. These provisions foresee the possibility that a number of Member States may establish among themselves enhanced cooperation in a specific area of the EU's structures.

[4] Commission, 'Proposal for a Council Decision authorising enhanced cooperation in the area of the creation of unitary patent protection' COM (2010) 790, containing the text of the proposal for the Council's decision and a detailed comment.

[5] Council Decision 2011/167/EU.

[6] On 30 May 2011, Italy and Spain announced that they had appealed to the European Court of Justice against the Council Decision of 10 March 2011 establishing enhanced cooperation in relation to the creation of unitary patent protection (Joined Cases C-274/11 and C-295/11). In its decision of 16 April 2013, the Court rejected the appeals and confirmed the validity of the Council Decision.

Pursuant to Article 20 TEU, enhanced cooperation may only be established under certain conditions.

First, enhanced cooperation may be established only 'within the framework of the Union's non-exclusive competences' and must be directed to 'further the objectives of the Union, protect its interests and reinforce its integration process'. Such cooperation is open at any time to all Member States (Article 20.1 TEU).

Second, two conditions must exist before the Council can adopt the decision authorising enhanced cooperation. On the one hand, the decision must be taken as a 'last resort, when it has established that the objectives of such cooperation cannot be attained within a reasonable period by the Union as a whole' and, on the other hand, when 'at least nine member States participate in it' (Article 20.2 TEU).

Title III of the TFEU reaffirms the principle that enhanced cooperation must 'comply with the Treaties and Union Law', must not 'undermine the internal market or economic, social and territorial cohesion' and must not constitute a barrier between Member States or distort competition between them. It must respect the competences and rights of the Member States not participating in it and, once established, must be open to all Member States (Articles 326–28). Title III finally specifies the procedure that interested Member States must follow to establish the cooperation among them (Articles 329–34).

From the provisions of Article 20 TEU and Title III of the TFEU, it is evident that enhanced cooperation is an exceptional measure to further the objectives of the EU in a particular area when unanimity is lacking among Member States, but where the determination exists among a group of Member States to cooperate in order to attain this objective. It is also evident that the conclusions reached at the Council meetings of 10 November and 10 December 2010 leave no doubt as to the lack of unanimity on the Commission's proposals concerning the translation arrangements, thus opening the way to enhanced cooperation.

The Council Decision of 10 March 2011 authorising enhanced cooperation for the creation of unitary patent protection is fully in line with the treaty provisions referred to above. However, a number of points in this decision should be highlighted, since they constitute the guidelines which will inspire the future efforts of the Member States within the framework of enhanced cooperation.

First, point 6 indicates that the creation of a unitary patent system in the participating Member States, which will ensure a uniform level of protection for inventions, should be seen as a move that will assist competition as well as a contribution to scientific and technological advances. The scope of these objectives is further developed in point 11 of the Decision.

Second, point 7 examines the question of the language regime as an essential element in the creation of a unitary system for the protection of inventions administered by the EPO. The central element in the functioning of such a regime is the translation arrangements, which should conform to the content of the Commission's proposal of 30 June 2010.[7] Patent applications should be filed with

[7] COM (2010) 350, (n 2).

the EPO in the language of any of the EU Member States and the costs relating to the translation of applications filed in languages other than an official language of the EPO (English, French and German) would be covered by a compensation scheme. The unitary patent would be granted in one of the official languages of the EPO.

Third, point 12 clarifies the scope of one of the main conditions for the establishment of enhanced cooperation, that is, that the unitary patent system is not included in the list of areas of exclusive competence of the EU as provided by Article 3.1 TEFU. Indeed, the legal basis for the creation of a European intellectual property title is, as already mentioned above, Article 118 TFEU, which specifically refers to the 'establishment and functioning of the internal market', which is a 'shared' competence of the EU pursuant to Article 4 TFEU. Therefore, the creation of a unitary patent system, including the applicable translation arrangements, falls within the EU's non-exclusive competence, thus satisfying the requirements set out in Article 20.1 TEU and Article 329.1 TFEU.

IV. The Debate on the Creation of a Unified Patent Litigation System: The Decision of the European Court of Justice on the Creation of a European Patent Court (2011)

As regards the creation of a unified patent litigation system, it should be noted first of all that since the 2000 Commission's proposal for a Council Regulation on the Community patent and during the subsequent negotiations, including the 2006 consultation, the debate on the proposed characteristics of such a system clearly showed that this was a complex question on which a range of diverging opinions of Member States and of potential users of the system existed. On one point, however, there seemed to be general agreement: that the high costs involved in the current multi-forum litigation system and the legal insecurity resulting from the risk of contradicting court decisions in different Member States should be resolved through the setting up of a unified jurisdictional system.

With this point in mind, the Commission proposed on 23 March 2009 the conclusion of a treaty among UE Member States and the other Member States of the EPO for the creation of a unified patent litigation system that would have jurisdiction over both European patents and future unitary patents.[8] With this proposal, the Commission reaffirmed its belief that the creation of such a

[8] Council Document 7927/09 of 23 March 2009. See also Council Document 7928/09 of 23 March 2009, which contained a recommendation by the Commission requesting the authorisation to negotiate the adoption of an agreement on the creation of a unitary patent litigation system for European and Community patents.

system was a necessary element of the unitary patent system and, in general, was a priority for Europe. It was evident that without the creation of a unified patent litigation system, the establishment of a unitary patent protection within the EU would result in a mere complementary procedure to that instituted by the EPC. The draft treaty was based on the procedure foreseen by Article 218 TFEU and took into account the central role that the EPO should have played within the framework of the future unitary patent and the results of the 2006 consultation. It provided for the creation of an integrated jurisdictional system for both European patents and future unitary patents. The court structure, established within the framework of the unified patent litigation system, would have jurisdiction concerning the infringement and validity of European and future unitary patents. The main features and tasks of the unified patent litigation system would involve a decentralised first instance and a single appeal instance, and would benefit from the role of the European Court of Justice in providing interpretation and application of EU law. The treaty would be complementary to the creation of a unitary patent, in the sense that the latter would not be able to operate without the parallel functioning of the unitary jurisdictional system.

In order to have legal certainty that the proposed draft treaty was compatible with EU law, it was deemed appropriate to ask the Court of Justice for an opinion under Article 218(11) TFEU and the Council presented the relevant request on 6 July 2009. In submitting the request, the Council, after having noted that 'a majority of [its members] believe that the envisaged agreement constitutes a legally possible way to achieve the envisaged aims', presented, individually, the observations of Member States on the draft treaty. These observations deserve to be considered, since they reflect a variety of positions among Member States and offer a panoramic view of their attitude towards the proposed treaty.

The observations may be summarised into four groups:

1) 'Observations on the admissibility of the request for an opinion': Ireland and Spain indicated that the Council request was premature, taking into account the stage reached by the preparatory works and in the process of negotiations.
2) 'Observations that the draft agreement is incompatible with the Treaties': Cyprus, Greece, Ireland, Italy, Lithuania, Luxembourg and Spain expressed the view (with different arguments and emphasis) that the draft treaty was incompatible with the principles and spirit of the EU Treaties, was lacking in terms of a legal basis and would create limits on the institutional powers assigned to the Court of Justice.
3) 'Observations that the draft agreement is incompatible with the Treaties unless alterations are made to the draft': the Parliament, the Commission, Belgium and France pointed out that notwithstanding the fact that the draft treaty appeared, in principle, to be compatible with the Treaties, it should be amended in order to guarantee the respect of the primacy of EU law by the Patent Court.
4) 'Observations that the draft agreement is compatible with the Treaties': the Czech Republic, Denmark, Estonia, Finland, Germany, the Netherlands,

> Poland, Portugal, Romania, Slovenia, Sweden and the UK expressed the opinion (with different qualifications) that the draft treaty as a whole appeared to be compatible with the Treaties.

On 8 March 2011, the Court of Justice issued the requested opinion.[9] It concluded that the proposed draft treaty was not compatible with the Treaties and with EU law in general. In summary, the Court indicated that conferring an exclusive jurisdiction in relation to a Community patent to an international institution—the European and Community Patents Court—which by definition is outside the institutional framework of the EU would deprive the national courts of Member States of their powers in relation to the interpretation and application of EU law. Consequently, the Court held that the draft treaty would alter the essential character of the powers conferred by the Treaties on the institutions of the EU and on the Member States, which are indispensable to the preservation of the very nature of EU law.

[9] Opinion 1/09 of 8 March 2011.

5

Carrying out the Enhanced Cooperation

I. The Council Decision of 10 March 2011 and the Opinion of the European Court of Justice of 8 March 2011

The Council Decision of 10 March 2011, which authorises enhanced cooperation for the creation of a unitary patent protection, and the opinion of the Court of Justice of 8 March 2011 on the draft treaty on a unified patent litigation system are the two acts which have contributed the most, each for different reasons, to the reopening of the debate on the adoption of a unitary patent system, thus overcoming the state of paralysis in which the negotiations stood in December 2010. On the one hand, even if enhanced cooperation constitutes an exceptional measure under EU law, the Decision of 10 March 2011, being an implicit declaration of political determination on the part of participating Member States to carry out the project on the unitary patent, stimulated a rapid and positive conclusion of the negotiations. On the other hand, the opinion of the Court of Justice of 8 March 2011 helped to clarify the legal basis for the preparation of an instrument setting up a unified patent litigation system compatible with the EU law.

II. Two Commission Proposals of 26 May 2011 in Relation to the Creation of Unitary Patent Protection and with Regard to the Applicable Translation Arrangements

In conformity with the Council decision which authorises enhanced cooperation, on 13 April 2011, the Commission adopted two proposals:

— A proposal for a Regulation of the European Parliament and of the Council implementing enhanced cooperation in relation to the creation of unitary patent protection.[1]

[1] Commission, 'Proposal for a Regulation of the European Parliament and of the Council implementing enhanced cooperation in the area of the creation of unitary patent protection' COM (2011) 0215.

— A proposal for a Council Regulation implementing enhanced cooperation in relation to the creation of unitary protection with regard to the applicable translation arrangements.[2]

The first proposal is based on Article 118(1) TFEU. Its aim is to offer the owner of a European patent under the EPC the possibility of requesting that such a patent benefits from unitary effect in the participating Member States. The unitary effect of a European patent consists in the unitary character of the title and in the granting of a uniform protection that has equal effect in the territories of the participating Member States. Such effect takes place in the participating Member States on the date of the publication by the EPO of the mention of the grant of the European patent. The requests for unitary effect for a European patent must be filed within one month after the mention of the grant is published in the European Patent Bulletin. It follows that all acts relating to a European patent with unitary effect, such as limitation, licence, transfer, revocation or lapse, have effect in respect of all participating Member States. Unitary effect is deemed not to have arisen to the extent that the European patent has been revoked or limited.

For the purposes of the administration of a European patent with unitary effect, the participating Member States confer to the EPO, pursuant to Article 143 EPC, a number of tasks. They relate, in particular, to the administration of requests for unitary effect, its registration in the European Patent Register, including any limitation, licence, transfer, revocation or lapse of the unitary patent, the collection of renewal fees and the distribution of part of the collected fees to the participating Member States and the administration of a compensation scheme of translation costs for European patent applications according to the provisions of the applicable translation arrangements.

The second proposal is based on Article 118(2) TFEU. This underlines the need that translation arrangements should be cost-effective and simplified and should ensure legal certainty. Such a regime should stimulate innovation and facilitate access to the European patent with unitary effect in an easy, less costly and less risky manner.[3] Since the EPO is responsible for the granting of European patents with unitary effect, the relevant translation arrangements should be built on the current procedure in the EPO, which implies the use of three languages: English, French and German. Where the claims of a European patent with unitary effect are published in the language of the proceedings before the EPO and include a translation in the other two official languages of the EPO in accordance with Article 14(6) of the EPC, no further translation is required. Further translations are requested in the event of a dispute and during a transitional period before a system of high-quality machine translations into all official languages of the EU

[2] Commission, 'Proposal for a Council Regulation implementing enhanced cooperation in the area of the creation of unitary patent protection with regard to the applicable translation arrangements' COM (2011) 0216.

[3] Commission, Proposal for a Council Regulation (EU) on the translation arrangements for the European Union patent' COM (2010) 350; see also Council Document 15385/10 of 9 November 2010.

becomes available. If not terminated beforehand by a decision of the Council, the transitional period automatically lapses 12 years after the Regulation becomes applicable. A compensation scheme of reimbursing translation costs, up to a fixed point for applicants filing patent applications in one of the official languages of the EU that is not an official language of the EPO, is entrusted to the EPO.

During May and June 2011, the two proposals were intensely debated by the delegations of participating Member States and were presented as compromise texts for adoption by the Council and the Parliament.[4] In December 2011, the Council and the Parliament expressed a provisional favourable opinion on the two Commission's proposals. It should be noted in this respect that the reports of the Legal Committee of the European Parliament of 9 and 11 January 2011 contain notations to the effect that these texts, notwithstanding a general consensus of participating Member States, did not yet constitute solutions which could be considered definitive as to the questions covered, in particular as far as the translation arrangements in the second proposal were concerned.

III. The Presidency Proposal of 26 May 2011 for the Resumption of Negotiations on the Creation of a Unified Patent Litigation System

Following the opinion issued by the European Court of Justice of 8 March 2011 declaring that the draft agreement on a unified patent litigation system prepared by the Commission was not compatible with the EU Treaties, the Hungarian Presidency proposed to the Council that the negotiations on the creation of a unitary jurisdiction on patent disputes should be resumed.[5] The basis for the discussion was an informal document issued by the Commission.[6] This proposed, as a possible negotiation platform, the conclusion of an international agreement, restricted to the Member States of the EU, on the creation of a unified court having jurisdiction in patent disputes in these States. The main features of the proposed jurisdiction would be as follows:

— a unitary court set up by Member States—the participation of third states should be excluded;
— an exclusive jurisdiction in patent disputes for European patents and European patents with unitary effect, with the purpose of avoiding duplication of jurisdiction;

[4] Council Document 11328/11 of 23 June 2011.
[5] Council Document 10630/11 of 26 May 2011.
[6] The text is contained in Annex II of Council Document 10630/11 of 26 May 2011.

— the main features of the unitary court should consist of a court of first instance, with local and central divisions, a court of appeal and a registry;
— a guarantee as to the full compliance on the part of the court with EU law.

These proposals were actively debated between May 2011 and October 2012; however, the results of these negotiations were divulged only in part. The negotiations produced a series of draft agreements having the declared aim of conforming with the opinion of the Court of Justice of 8 March 2011 and in general with EU law.[7] Notwithstanding the fact that these drafts achieved a general consensus, they did not yet constitute an agreed text of this instrument. Its final adoption was linked, on the one hand, to the clarification of a number of technical questions relating to the application of the agreement and, on the other hand, to a preliminary political compromise on the so-called 'patent package' composed of the text of the agreement and of the texts of the regulations on unitary patent protection and on translation arrangements.

In turn, however, the adoption of the patent package was dependent on the still unresolved question of the location of the seat of the unified jurisdiction. In June 2012, this delicate and complex question was finally answered. On the occasion of the Council meeting of 28 and 29 June 2012, it was decided that the Central Division of the Court of First Instance, within the Unified Patent Court (UPC), together with the office of the President of the Court of First Instance should be located in Paris and that the first President of the Court of First Instance should be of French nationality. In order to balance this decision from a geopolitical point of view and taking into account the highly specialised nature of patent disputes, the decision was also taken to create two sections of the Central Division: one in London and the other in Munich.[8]

IV. Agreement on the 'Patent Package': Approval by the European Parliament on 11 December 2012

Once the delicate question of the seat of the Court of First Instance was resolved, the negotiations for the reaching of an agreement on the so-called 'patent package' accelerated its rhythm. The package included the following texts:

— a draft Regulation on translation arrangements;[9]
— a draft consolidated version of the UPC Agreement;[10]

[7] See the following Council documents, which summarise the status of the negotiations during this period: Document 11533/11 of 14 June 12011; Document 13751/11 of 2 September 2011; Document 18239/11, not published; Document 10059/11 of 24 May 2012; Document 14750/11 of 12 October 2012. This latter document contains the consolidated text at the date of publication of the draft Agreement on the Unitary Patent Court (UPC) and the draft Statute of the Court.

[8] Council Document EUCO 76/12 of 29 June 2012.

[9] Council Document 18855/11 of 13 November 2012.

[10] Council Document 16221/12 of 14 November 2012.

- a draft Declaration of the Contracting Member States concerning the preparations for the coming into force of the UPC Agreement;[11]
- a proposed text for a new Article 5 and the deletion of Articles 6–8 of the draft Regulation on unitary patent protection;[12]
- a draft joint statement by the participating Member States concerning the share of distribution among themselves of renewal fees for European patents with unitary effect.[13]

The Permanent Representatives Committee reached an agreement on these texts on 19 November 2012 and accordingly informed the European Parliament Legal Committee, indicating that the vast majority of its members were in favour of a rapid conclusion of the negotiations on the basis of the package.[14] In its plenary session of 11 December 2012, the European Parliament adopted with three separate Resolutions,[15] based on three corresponding Reports[16] of the Legal Committee, the following:

- a proposal for a Regulation of the European Parliament and of the Council implementing enhanced cooperation in relation to the creation of unitary patent protection;
- a proposal for a Council Regulation implementing enhanced cooperation in relation to the creation of unitary patent protection with regard to the applicable translations arrangements;
- the setting up of a jurisdictional system for patent disputes, based on an international agreement among the participating Member States for the creation of a unified patent court.

After 12 years of long and complex negotiations, which started in Lisbon on 24 March 2000, the setting up of a unitary patent system within the EU was finally adopted.

[11] Council Document 16222/12 of 14 November 2012.

[12] For the text of the new draft art 5, see Annex I, Council Document 16220/12 of 14 November 2012.

[13] For the text of the draft declaration, see Annex II, Council Document 16220/12 of 14 November 2012.

[14] Council Document 16749/12 of 4 December 2012.

[15] European Parliament Legislative Resolution of 11 December 2012 on the Proposal for a Regulation of the European Parliament and of the Council Implementing Enhanced Cooperation in the Area of the Creation of a Unitary Patent Protection (COM (2011) 0215-C7-0099/2011–2011/0093 (COD)).

European Parliament Legislative Resolution of 11 December 2012 on the Proposal for a Council Regulation Implementing Enhanced Cooperation in the Area of the Creation of a Unitary Patent Protection with regard to Translation Arrangements (COM (2011) 0216-C7-0145/2011—2011/0094 (CNS)).

European Parliament Legislative Resolution of 11 December 2012 on Jurisdictional System for Patent Disputes (2011/2176(INI)).

[16] Report on the proposal of the European Parliament and the Council Implementing Enhanced Cooperation in the Area of the Creation of Unitary Patent Protection-Rapporteur: Bernard Rapkay (A7-0001/2012).

Report on the proposal for a Council Regulation Implementing Enhanced Cooperation in the Area of Unitary Patent Protection with Regard to Translation Arrangements-Rapporteur: Raffaele Baldassarre (A7-0002/2012).

Report on a Jurisdictional System for Patent Disputes-Rapporteur: Klaus-Heiner Lehene (A7-0009/2012).

6

The European Patent with Unitary Effect

I. Introduction: The Legal Nature of the Regulations

The legislative Resolutions of the European Parliament of 11 December 2012 gave rise to the setting up of a unitary patent system within the EU based on the following instruments:

- Regulation (EU) 1257/2012 of the European Parliament and of the Council of 17 December 2012 implementing enhanced cooperation in the area of the creation of unitary patent protection.[1]
- Regulation (EU) 1260/2012 of the Council of 17 December 2012 implementing enhanced cooperation in the area of the creation of unitary patent protection with regard to the applicable translations arrangements.[2]
- The Agreement on a Unified Patent Court (UPC) and the Statute of the Court.[3]

The texts of the two Regulations and of the UPC Agreement are reproduced in Appendices I, II and III, respectively.

Before examining the legal mechanism set up by these acts in detail, it is necessary to consider a number of aspects peculiar to their nature and their interrelationships.

First, it should be noted that the instruments which make up the system of the European patent with unitary effect present, according to their legal nature, different characteristics and functions, which are the result of very specific and difficult negotiation choices: two are EU Regulations, while the other is an international agreement. The Regulation is a primary source of EU law. It has a direct effect on the legal system of each Member State, like a national law. The provisions of an international agreement apply in those Member States that have ratified the agreement or have adhered to it in conformity with the provisions of their respective national laws and pursuant to the prescribed formalities.

[1] OJ L361/1 of 31 December 2012.
[2] OJ L361/89 of 31 December 2012.
[3] Council Document 16351/12 of 11 January 2012.

Second, it should be pointed out that because of the different legal nature of the three instruments referred to above, a discrepancy existed in relation to the time of their applicability which, if not duly taken into account, would have jeopardised the practical functioning of the entire system. The two Regulations were published on 31 December 2012 in the Official Journal of the European Union and entered into force 20 days after their publication, that is, on 20 January 2013. The entry into force of the Agreement on a Unified Patent Court is foreseen to take place according to the following conditions provided for in its Article 89(1):

— on 1 January 2014; or
— on the first day of the fourth month after the deposit of the thirteenth instrument of ratification or accession, including the three Member States[4] in which the highest number of European patents had effect in the year preceding that in which the signature of the Agreement takes place; or
— on the first day of the fourth month after the day of entry into force of the amendments to Regulation (EU) 1215/2012 concerning its relationship with the Agreement; or
— whichever of the said dates is the latest.

In simplified terms, these conditions mean that the UPC will enter into force when at least 13 contracting states have ratified it, including France, Germany and the UK, the three states in which the highest number of European patents had effect in 2012, and when the required amendments to Regulation (EU) 1215/2012 on jurisdiction, recognition and enforcement of judgments in civil and commercial matters enter into force, whichever of the corresponding dates is the latest.

In order to enable the contemporary applicability of the three acts and therefore the full functioning of the unitary patent system, the relevant instruments have been connected to each other under the mechanism provided by Article 89(1) of the UPC, which can be defined as a 'time' mechanism. Indeed, Regulations (EU) 1257/2012 and (EU) 1260/2012 provide, respectively, in Articles 18.2 and 7.2 that—even if in force—they will be applicable only as of 1 January 2014 or as of the date of entry into force of the UPC Agreement, whichever is the later date. In this regard, it should be noted that, notwithstanding the fact that the unitary patent system and the UPC are inseparable elements, the solution offered by this mechanism introduces an element of uncertainty into the functioning of the whole unitary patent system, since its actual working depends exclusively on the entry into force of one of the three acts on which it is based. Indeed, as for any international treaty, the entry into force of the UPC essentially depends on the decision of its contracting states to ratify it. This means that the UPC contracting states could theoretically delay *sine die* the beginning of the operation of the system, thus nullifying the success of the adoption of the three instruments by the European Parliament of 12 December 2012.

[4] France, Germany and the UK.

The UPC Agreement was signed in Brussels by 25 EU Member States on 19 February 2013. Croatia, Poland and Spain did not sign the Agreement (Croatia only became an EU Member State in July 2013). Italy signed the Agreement although it is not participating in the enhanced cooperation regime.

II. Regulation (EU) 1257/2012 of 17 December 2012

A. The Legal Basis and Structure of the Regulation

Regulation (EU) 1257/2012 of the European Parliament and of the Council of 17 December 2012 establishes a unitary patent system within the EU, applying Council Decision 2011/167/EU, which authorises enhanced cooperation in this area. It will therefore be applicable in the Member States participating in such cooperation. As previously indicated, the legal basis of the Regulation is Article 118(1) TFEU. The Regulation constitutes:

- — a special agreement within the meaning of Article 142 of the EPC of 5 October 1973, which was revised on 17 December 1991 and 29 November 2000;
- — a regional patent treaty within the meaning of Article 45(1) of the PCT of 19 June 1970, which was last modified on 3 February 2001;
- — a special agreement within the meaning of Article 19 of the Paris Convention of 20 March 1883, which was last amended on 28 September 1979.

These qualifications imply that the provisions of the Regulation should not contradict the provisions of the three above-mentioned international instruments.

The structure of the Regulation is subdivided into four chapters of substantive provisions and two chapters of financial and final provisions. The substantial provisions deal with the functioning of the unitary patent system. They specify the nature and the mechanism of the unitary effect from which a European patent may benefit upon request by its owner, the scope of the rights conferred by the patent with unitary effect, the conditions for treating a European patent with unitary effect as a national patent and the tasks to be undertaken by the EPO in administering the unitary patent system.

B. Unitary Effect

A European patent pursuant to the EPC granted with the same claims in all participating Member States benefits from unitary effect in these States upon the request of its owner and provided that it is registered in the Register for unitary patent protection kept by the EPO. The European patent with unitary effect has a unitary character in the sense that it grants to the owner a uniform protection and has equal effect in all participating Member States. The unitary character implies that any limitation, transfer, revocation or lapse takes place in respect of all participating Member States, although with the proviso that any licence grant may be limited to a part of the territories of the participating Member States and that the unitary effect is deemed not to have arisen if the European patent has been revoked or limited (Article 3).

C. Effect of Registration

The effect of the unitary patent in the territories of the participating Member States dates from the publication date by the EPO of the mention of the granting of the European patent in the *European Patent Bulletin*. Where the unitary effect of a European patent has been registered as prescribed, the participating Member States take the necessary measures to ensure that the European patent is deemed not to have effect as a national patent in their territory on the date of publication of the mention of the grant (Article 4).

D. Rights Conferred

The rights conferred by the European patent with unitary effect to its owner consist of the right to prevent third parties from committing any act against which the patent provides protection in the territories of the participating Member States in which it has unitary effect, subject to the applicable limitations. The scope of these rights and its limitations are uniform across the aforementioned Member States. The definition of the acts against which the patent provides protection and the applicable limitations is left to the national provisions applicable to European patents with unitary effects in the participating Member State whose national law applies to the unitary patent as an object of property (Article 5).

The rights conferred do not extend to acts relating to a product protected by the unitary patent carried out in the participating Member States after the product has been introduced in the territory of the EU by or with the consent of the owner, unless he has valid reasons to oppose further commercialisation of the product (Article 6).

E. The Unitary Patent as an Object of Property

A European patent with unitary effect as an object of property is treated in its entirety and in all participating Member States as a national patent of the State in which the patent has unitary effect and in which the applicant had his residence or principal place of business at the date of the filing of the European patent application (Article 7).

The patent owner, who is prepared to allow any person to use the patented invention as a licensee, may file with the EPO a statement to that effect and the licence is treated as a contractual licence (Article 8).

F. Administration of the Unitary Patent

The administration of the European patent with unitary effect is conferred by the participating Member States to the EPO, pursuant to Article 143 of the EPC, to carry on a number of tasks in accordance with the internal rules of the EPO. These tasks consist of administering requests for unitary effect, to include the Register for unitary patent protection within the European Patent Register and administer this Register, to ensure that a request for unitary effect is presented in the language of the proceedings within a month of publication of the mention of the grant in the European Patent Bulletin and to ensure that unitary effect is indicated in the Register for unitary patent protection and, during the transitional period under Article 6 of Regulation (EU) 1260/2012, that the request is accompanied by the prescribed translations. Furthermore, the EPO is responsible for receiving statements on licensing, collecting and administering renewal and additional fees, as well as distributing part of the collected renewal fees to the participating Member States and administering the compensation scheme for reimbursement of translation costs pursuant to Article 5 of Regulation (EU) 1260/2012.

In the framework of the obligations undertaken by the participating Member States in their capacity of contracting states of the EPC, they ensure compliance with the Regulation and, to that end, they have set up a Select Committee of the Administrative Council of the EPO pursuant to Article 145 of the EPC (Article 9).[5]

G. Financial and Final Provisions: Entry into Force

In addition to the substantive provisions examined, the Regulation contains two groups of norms regulating the financial aspects of the unitary patent system and setting forth the so-called final provisions.

The financial provisions relate, on the one hand, to renewal fees for European patents with unitary effect (Articles 10–12) and, on the other hand, to the distribution of part of the collected fees to the participating Member States (Article 13). In this respect, it should be pointed out that the EPO's expenses incurred in carrying out the additional tasks given to it by the participating Member States pursuant to Article 143 of the EPC are covered by the fees generated by the unitary patents.

The renewal fees are due for the years following that in which the mention of the granting of the European patent with unitary effect is published in the

[5] The Select Committee was established by the participating Member States on 20 March 2013. The said Committee deals, inter alia, with the preparation of draft Rules to implement the tasks entrusted to the EPO, which are referred to as Rules Relating to Unitary Patent Protection and are currently under discussion.

European Patent Bulletin. If they are not paid in due course, the patent lapses. The renewal fees are progressive throughout the term of the unitary patent protection and its level is fixed with the aim of facilitating innovation and fostering competitiveness of European enterprises, in particular small and medium-sized enterprises (SMEs).

The EPO retains 50 per cent of the renewal fees to cover all costs associated with the tasks conferred on it by the participating Member States and distributes the remaining part to the aforementioned States. The distribution share is based on the number of patent applications, on the size of the market and on a compensation to the participating Member States which have an official language that is not one of the EPO official languages and a level of patent activity that is particularly low.

The final provisions consist of norms relating to the cooperation between the Commission and the EPO, as well as the participating Member States (Articles 14–17) and concerning the entry into force and application of the Regulation, including the prescriptions for the ratification of the UPC by the participating Member States (Article 18).

The Commission has established close cooperation with the EPO, through a working agreement, in the fields covered by the Regulation, particularly those relating to the issue of renewal fees. As to the general functioning of the Regulation, at regular intervals, the Commission presents to the European Parliament and the Council a report on its operation, formulating, where necessary, proposals for amendments. In their turn, the participating Member States inform the Commission by the date of application of the Regulation on the measures adopted pursuant to Articles 4(2) and 9.

As previously noted, the Regulation makes a distinction between the 'entry into force' and 'application' of its provisions. It enters into force 20 days following its publication in the Official Journal of the European Union, that is, on 20 January 2014, while its application is deferred to a later date: 1 January 2014 or the date of the entry into force of the UPC, whichever is the later. It follows from these rules that by way of derogation from Articles 3(1) and (2) and 4(1), a European patent with unitary effect deploys this effect only in the participating Member States in which the UPC has exclusive jurisdiction with regard to European patents having unitary effect at the date of registration, it being understood that unitary patent protection may be requested for any European patent granted on or after the date of application of the Regulation.

When depositing the instrument of ratification of the UPC, each Member State notifies the relevant ratification to the Commission. The Commission publishes in the Official Journal of the European Union the date of entry into force of the Agreement and a list of the Member States that have ratified the Agreement at that date. Thereafter, it updates this list and publishes it.

III. Regulation (EU) 1260/2012 of 17 December 2012

A. Legal Basis

Council Regulation (EU) 1260/2012 of 17 December 2012 completes the substantial provisions of Regulation (EU) 1257/2012 of the same date. It regulates a specific aspect of the implementation of the enhanced cooperation for the creation of unitary patent protection—that relating to translation arrangements for European patents with unitary effect—and deals with a number of specific situations relating to the application of the translation regime, provided for in Regulation 1257/2012.

As previously indicated, the legal basis of the Regulation is Article 118(2) TFEU and its declared aim is the setting up of a uniform translations regime for European patents that has unitary effect and is simple and cost-effective. Such a regime should ensure legal certainty and stimulate innovation, and making access to unitary patent protection easier, less costly and legally secure should in particular benefit SMEs.

B. Situations Covered

The Regulation covers three situations in connection with translation arrangements:

— for a European patent with unitary effect;
— in the event of a dispute;
— in the event of administration of a compensation scheme.

In the first situation, no further translations are required where the specification of a unitary patent has been published in accordance with Article 14(6) of the EPC, it being understood that the request for unitary effect pursuant to Article 9 of Regulation (EU) 1257/2012 must be submitted in the language of the proceedings.

In the second situation, a full translation of the European patent with unitary effect must be provided upon request in three circumstances: in the event of a dispute relating to an alleged infringement of the unitary patent; in the event of a dispute relating to a unitary patent; and in the event of a dispute concerning a claim for damages. In the first instance, the patent owner must provide, at the request and choice of an alleged infringer, a translation of the unitary patent into an official language of either the participating Member State in which the alleged infringement took place or the Member State where the alleged infringer is domiciled. In the second instance, the translation must be provided in the course of legal proceedings, at the request of the competent court, in the language used in the proceedings before that court. In the first and second instances, the cost of the translations is borne by the patent owner. In the third instance, the court hearing the dispute, before requesting the translation of the unitary patent into an official language of either the participating Member State in which the alleged infringement took place or the Member State where the alleged infringer is domiciled, takes into account (in particular where the alleged infringer is an SME, a person, a not-for-profit entity, a university or public research organisation) whether the alleged infringer acted without knowing that he was infringing the unitary patent (Article 4).

With a view to assisting applicants filing patent applications at the EPO in one of the official language of the EU that is not an official language of the EPO, the participating Member States, in accordance with Article 9 of Regulation (EU) 1257/2012, give the EPO, within the meaning of Article 143 of the EPC, the task of administering a compensation scheme for the reimbursement of translation costs, up to a ceiling, of such patent applications. The compensation scheme is funded by the renewal fees for unitary patents and is available to SMEs, persons, not-for-profit entities, universities and public research organisations that have their place of residence in a Member State (Article 5).

The rules examined above are integrated by a number of norms which regulate, on the one hand, the submission of requests for unitary effect during a transitional period and, on the other hand, specify the modalities and conditions for the entry into force and the applicability of the Regulation.

The transitional period starts from the date of the application of the Regulation and, unless terminated on the basis of a proposal by the Commission, it lapses 12 years after the date of its application. During this period, a request for unitary effect is accompanied by an English translation of the specification of the unitary patent if the language of the proceedings is French or German or, where the language of the proceedings is English, by a translation in any other official language of the EU. The text of these translations is published by the EPO as soon as possible after the date of the request for unitary effect, it being understood that the texts of these translations have no legal effect, but only perform the function of providing information.

An independent expert committee, established by the participating Member States in the framework of the EPO and composed of representatives of the non-governmental organisations representing the users of the unitary patent system, carries out, six years after the date of application of the Regulation and every two years thereafter, an objective evaluation of the availability of high-quality translation machines as developed by the EPO. On the basis of these evaluations, the Commission presents a report to the Council and, if appropriate, proposes the termination of the transitional period (Article 6).

As in the case of Regulation 1257/2012, the Regulation makes a distinction between 'entry into force' and 'applicability', so that the two instruments are aligned in this respect. The Regulation enters into force 20 days after its publication in the Official Journal of the European Union, which means that it entered into force, like Regulation 1257/2012, on 20 January 2013, while its applicability is deferred to a later date: 1 January 2014 or the date of entry into force of the UPC Agreement, whichever date is the later (Article 7).

IV. Conclusion

The provisions of Regulations (EU) 1257/2012 and 1260/2012 confirm that the legal structure of the European patent system with unitary effect gives rise to two main considerations. First, the new system offers a 'third way' for the protection of inventions in Europe besides the protection granted by national patents and by that conferred by the European patent under the EPC, both of which continue to be accessible. Second, the system proves that it derives directly from a legal and administrative point of view from the EPC.

As regards the first aspect, the creation and the availability of a 'corpus' of unitary patent norms applicable in the territory of the participating Member States helps enterprises to modulate their production activities and therefore to ameliorate the quality of strategic decisions aimed at a more efficient distribution of products in the internal market. This substantially contributes to the attainment of the objectives of the EU, as set out in Article 3(3) TEU. Indeed, if a uniform patent protection constitutes a general incentive for the development of new technological solutions for enterprises which operate in the internal market, this means an additional immediate benefit in terms of reduction of costs and increased legal certainty, thus elevating the level of their competitiveness.

Concerning the second aspect, the creation of the European patent with unitary effect determines not only a further substantial legal integration of the national patent provisions of the participating Member States, but also a development of the legal and administrative scope of the EPC norms and an enlargement of the tasks of the EPO. The fulcrum of this development, as regards the relationship of the EPO with the unitary patent system, is constituted by the interaction of the tasks of the EPO set forth in Articles 9–11, 13 and 14 of Regulation (EU) 1257/2012. This interaction designs a unitary system for the protection of inventions within the EU which is firmly rooted in the EPC and widens the scope of its applicability through a number of specific administrative tasks conferred by the participating Member States on the EPO. The involvement of the EPO in the functioning of the unitary patent system is further substantiated by the creation on 20 March 2013 of the Select Committee of the Administrative Council of the EPO, which has the task of ensuring the governance and supervision of activities related to the tasks set forth in particular in Articles 9 and 12–13 of Regulation (EU) 1257/2012.

Furthermore, the fact that the European unitary patent system is embedded, to a large extent, in the European patent system under the EPC stems from the provisions of Regulation (EU) 1260/2012. This Regulation, which establishes a translation regime for unitary patents, confirms the use of the trilingual system in force in the proceedings under the EPC. As previously outlined, the question of the translation regime has largely dominated the negotiations for the adoption of a unitary patent system and it became evident that it could be solved by adopting the language system in force under the EPC.

Finally, it should be noted that the enlargement of the legal and administrative scope of the EPC confirms the 'vitality' of the Convention adopted in Munich in 1973 and its harmonising function of the European patent legislations.

7

The Unified Patent Court

I. Introduction

The legal structure of the unitary patent jurisdiction is based on two interlinked instruments: the UPC Agreement and the Statute of the Court, which is contained in Annex I of the UPC Agreement.[1] The two instruments interact in relation to the organisation of the Court, its competence and the procedural provisions. This structure is completed, as provided for in Article 41 of the UPC, by the Rules of Procedure to be prepared by the Preparatory Committee of the UPC and to be adopted by the Administrative Committee established under Article 12 of the UPC.

The Agreement is composed of five parts in which two categories of substantive norms prevail: the institutional and the organisation and procedural provisions. Where necessary, the scope and practical application of these norms are further specified in the corresponding provisions of the Statute. The normative framework is completed by financial, transitory and final provisions.

The present chapter examines in particular the substantive provisions of the UPC, that is, the general and institutional provisions (Part I, Articles 1–35), the organisational and institutional provisions (Part II, Articles 40–82), the transitional provisions (Part IV, Article 83) and the final provisions (Part V, Articles 84–89).

II. The UPC Agreement and the Statute

A. General and Institutional Provisions

Before examining the main characteristics of the jurisdictional system set up by the UPC Agreement, it should be pointed out that the UPC is a court for the settlement of disputes relating to European patents and European patents with unitary effect that is common to the contracting Member States of the Agreement and thus is part of their judicial system (Article 1 of the Agreement). The scope

[1] Council Document 16351/12 of 11 January 2013.

of the Agreement covers European patents with unitary effect, European patents still in force at the date of entry into force of the Agreement or granted after that date and European patent applications pending at the date of the entry into force of the Agreement or filed after that date (Article 3 of the Agreement). The Court has a legal personality in each contracting Member State and is represented by the President of the Court of Appeal (Article 4 of the Agreement).

The Court is made up of three institutions:

— a Court of First Instance;
— a Court of Appeal; and
— a Registry.

It comprises both legally qualified and technically qualified judges. The former possess the qualifications required by a contracting Member State to carry on jurisdictional functions, while the latter have a university degree, a specific expertise in a technological field and a proven legal and procedural knowledge in patent litigation (Article 15 of the Agreement; Chapter I of the Statute).

The management of the Court is conferred to a Presidium, comprising the President and two judges of the Court of Appeal, by the President and three judges of the Court of First Instance, and by the Registrar (Article 15 of the Statute).

Responsibility for the implementation of the Agreement is conferred on an Administrative Committee, a Budget Committee and an Advisory Committee (Articles 12–14 of the Agreement).

i. The Court of First Instance

The Court of First Instance comprises a central division and local and regional divisions. As has already been indicated, the seat of the central division is in Paris, with sections in London and Munich (Article 7(1) and (2) of the Agreement). The central division and its two sections are competent for the following cases in accordance with the International Patent Classification:[2]

— Paris seat: five cases—performing operations and transporting; textiles and paper; fixed constructions; physics; and electricity;
— London section: two cases—human necessities; and chemistry and metallurgy;
— Munich section: one case—mechanical, engineering, lighting, heating, weapons, blasting (Annex II of the Agreement).

The President of the Court of First Instance is elected by all its judges for a period of three years and may be re-elected twice. The first President is a national of

[2] The International Patent Classification (IPC) is established under the Strasbourg Agreement Concerning the International Patent Classification of 24 May 1971, which was modified on 28 September 1979. The Strasbourg Agreement is administered by the WIPO. This Agreement subdivides the technical fields into eight main sections and about 67, 000 subdivisions. Each of these subdivisions is identified by a symbol composed of Arabic numerals and by letters of the Latin alphabet. The appropriate symbol is indicated on each patent document by the national or regional industrial property office which publishes the document.

the contracting Member State that hosts the central division (Article 14 of the Statute).[3]

Each Contracting Member State may request the setting up in its territory of a local division pursuant to the procedure provided for in the Statute. The number of local divisions in a contracting Member State cannot exceed four. Upon the request of two or more contracting Member States, a regional division may be set up in the aforementioned States according to the procedure provided for in the Statute. The regional division may hear cases in several locations (Article 7(3)–(5) of the Agreement; Article 18 of the Statute).

The panels of the Court of First Instance are composed of three judges. Any panel of the central division is composed of two legally qualified judges from different contracting Member States and by one technically qualified judge nominated by the pool of judges.

The panels of a local division in a contracting Member State where, during three consecutive years prior or subsequent to the entry into force of the Agreement, fewer than 50 cases per year have been commenced, are composed of one legally qualified judge from that State and by two legally qualified judges who are not nationals of the aforementioned State nominated by the pool of judges. In such a division, where the number of cases commenced is 50 or more per calendar year, the relevant panels are made up of two legally qualified judges from the State concerned and one legally qualified judge who is not a national of that State and is allocated by the pool of judges.

The panels of a regional division are composed of two legally qualified judges, chosen from a regional list, who are nationals of the contracting Member States concerned and by one legally qualified judge who is not a national of these States and is allocated by the pool of judges (Article 8 of the Agreement; Article 19 of the Statute).

The pool of judges includes all legally and technically qualified judges of the Court of First Instance. These judges may be allocated by the President of the Court of First Instance to the relevant division on the basis of their respective legal and technical qualifications (Article 18 of the Agreement; Article 20 of the Statute).

ii. The Court of Appeal

The Court of Appeal has its seat in Luxembourg. It is presided over by a President who is elected using the same procedure as that for the election of the President of the Court of First Instance. Its panels are composed of five judges: three legally qualified judges from different contracting Member States and two technically qualified judges allocated by the pool of judges. Any panel of the Court of Appeal is presided over by a legally qualified judge (Article 9 of the Agreement; Article 13 of the Statute).

[3] As indicated in section III of ch 5, during the Council meeting of 28 and 29 June 2012, it was decided that the first President of the Court of First Instance would be of French nationality.

iii. The Registry

The Registry is set up at the seat of the Court of Appeal, with subregistries in all divisions of the Court of First Instance.

The Registrar is appointed by the Presidium for a period of six years, which may be renewed. It assists the Court, the President of the Court of Appeal, the President of the Court of First Instance and the judges in performing their duties. The Registrar is responsible for the organisation and activities of the Registry, for the keeping of the Register, including the records of all cases before the Court, for the keeping and administering of the lists of judges who make up the pool of judges for the lists of European Patent Attorneys authorised to act before the Court and the lists of court experts, and for the publication of notifications, withdrawals, decisions of the Court and the annual statistical data. The organisation and activities of subregistries are managed by the Deputy Registrar (Article 10 of the Agreement; Articles 22–25 of the Statute).

iv. Primacy of EU Law, Sources of Law and Substantive Law

After having specified the composition and structure of the institutions forming the UPC, the Agreement deals with the legal principles on which the jurisdictional activity of the Court is based. First, the principle of the primacy of EU law is confirmed, which the Court must fully apply and respect, and, second, the sources of law on which the Court bases its decisions are enumerated. Furthermore, the elements of substantive law to be taken into account in the screening of cases submitted to the Court are indicated.

Concerning the first aspect, the Court, as an institution common to the contracting Member States and part of their judicial system, must cooperate with the Court of Justice of the European Union to ensure the correct application and uniform interpretation of EU law in accordance with the provisions of Article 267 TFEU (Articles 20 and 21 of the Agreement). It follows that pursuant to EU law concerning non-contractual liability of Member States for damages caused by their national courts violating EU law, the contracting Member States are jointly liable for damages resulting from the infringement of EU law by the Court of Appeal. The actions for damages must be brought against the contracting Member State where the claimant has its residence or principal place of business or, in their absence, before the competent authority of that State. The claimant has the right to obtain the entire amount of damages claimed from the Member State against which the action was brought. The contracting Member State that has paid damages has the right to request a proportional contribution from the other Member States in conformity with the applicable modalities established by the Administrative Committee. Actions of the Court are attributable to each Member State individually as well as collectively to all Member States (Articles 22 and 23 of the Agreement).

As regards the second aspect, the Agreement specifies that, notwithstanding the full compliance with the principle of primacy of EU law, the Court bases its decisions on:

- EU law, including Regulations (EU) 1257/2012 and 1260/2012;
- the provisions of the UPC Agreement;
- the provisions of the EPC;
- international patent instruments applicable to all contracting Member States; and
- national law (Article 24 of the Agreement).

With respect to the third aspect, the Agreement recalls the principal substantive provisions in most national legislation relating to the rights conferred to the patent owner, such as the right to prevent any non-authorised third party from directly and indirectly using the patented invention, the limitations of the effects of a patent, the rights based on prior use of the invention, the exhaustion of the rights conferred by a European patent and the scope of the rights conferred by supplementary protection certificates. These norms are integrated by appropriate references to the applicable international conventions and to the relevant EU Directives and Regulations (Articles 25–30 of the Agreement).

v. International Jurisdiction and Competence

The international jurisdiction of the Court is established pursuant to Regulation (EU) 1215/2012 of 12 December 2012 or, where applicable, on the basis of the Lugano Convention of 30 October 2007, both on jurisdiction and the recognition and enforcement of judgments in civil and commercial matters (Article 31 of the Agreement).[4]

The Court has exclusive competence in respect of a number of actions, each before a specific jurisdictional organ, with the proviso that the national courts of the contracting Member States remain competent for actions which do not fall within the exclusive competence of the Court. The main features of such actions may be described as follows:

- actions for:

  actual or threatened infringement of patents and supplementary protection certificates, including counterclaims concerning licences,
  provisional and protective measures and injunctions,
  damages on the basis of a published European patent application,
  the use of the invention prior to the granting of the patent or to the right based on prior use of the invention,

[4] See ch 8 below.

must be brought before the local division in the Contracting Member State where the actual or threatened infringement has occurred or may occur, or before the local division where the defendant has its residence, its principal place of business or its place of business, or the regional division in which the Member State participates;

- actions for compensation for licences on the basis of Article 8 of Regulation (EU) 1257/2012 must be brought before the local or regional division of the contracting Member State where the defendant has its residence, its principal place of business or place of business;
- actions for declaration of non-infringement of patents and supplementary patent certificates, of revocation of patents and for declaration of invalidity of supplementary patent certificates must be brought before the central division;
- counterclaims for a revocation of patents and for a declaration of invalidity of supplementary patent certificates;
- a counterclaim for revocation may be brought in the case of an action for infringement referred to in Article 32(1)(a); in such a case, the local or regional division concerned has the discretion, after having heard the claims of the parties, either to proceed with both the action for infringement and the counterclaim for revocation, to refer the counterclaim for revocation to the central division and suspend or proceed with the action for infringement or refer the case, with the consent of the parties, to the central division (see Article 33(3) of the Agreement);
- actions concerning decisions of the EPO in carrying out the tasks referred to in Article 9 of Regulation (EU) 1257/2012 must be brought before the central division (Articles 32 and 33 of the Agreement).

vi. Patent Mediation and Arbitration

Mediation and arbitration in patent disputes are provided for by a Mediation and Arbitration Centre, which has seats in Ljubljana and Lisbon. It provides assistance in patent disputes within the scope of the Agreement. The provisions of Article 82 on the enforcement of decisions and orders apply *mutatis mutandis* to the settlement of disputes achieved through the activities of the Centre, with the proviso that a patent cannot be revoked or limited as a consequence of mediation and arbitration proceedings (Article 35 of the Agreement).

B. Organisational and Procedural Provisions

The norms relating to the organisation and functioning of the Court constitute the central part of the structure of the Agreement. The procedural details of these norms are developed in Rules of Procedure to be established under Article 41 of the Agreement.[5] Concerning the general structure of the organisational and

[5] See ch 8.

procedural provisions, it should be noted that these provisions are inspired, to a large extent, by those of the national judicial systems. Thus, the resulting general framework is that of a unitary organisation and procedural system that synthesise principles, rules and procedures of national systems.

i. Legal Capacity

Any natural person or legal entity entitled under national law to initiate proceedings has the capacity to bring actions before the Court. The patent owner, the holder of an exclusive licence in respect to a patent, unless the licence agreement provides otherwise, and the holder of a non-exclusive licence, if expressly permitted to do so by the licensing agreement, are entitled to bring actions before the Court (Articles 46 and 47 of the Agreement).

ii. Representation

Parties are represented before the Court by lawyers authorised to practise before a Court pursuant to the national law of a contracting Member State or by European patent attorneys entitled to act before the EPO under Article 134 of the EPC (Article 48 of the Agreement).

iii. Language of Proceedings

Before any local or regional division of the Court of First Instance, the language of the proceedings is an official language of the EU which is the official language, respectively, of the contracting Member State hosting the relevant division or designated by the Member State sharing a regional division. However, contracting Member States may designate as the language of the proceedings of their local or regional division one or more of the official languages of the EPO.

In the following cases, the language of the proceedings is the language in which the patent was granted:

— when, subject to the approval of the competent panel, the parties agree to use such language;
— if the competent panel, with the agreement of the parties, decides to use such language;
— when the President of the Court of First Instance, upon the request of one of the parties and after having heard the other parties and the competent panel, decides to use such language;
— in the proceedings before the central division.

The language of the proceedings before the Court of Appeal is the language before the Court of First Instance; however, the parties may agree on the use of the language in which the patent was granted.

Under specific circumstances, upon request of the parties, interpretation and translation facilities may be agreed upon (Articles 49–51 of the Agreement).

iv. Proceedings before the Court

In the proceedings before the Court, the Agreement distinguishes between the procedures admitted before the Court, in accordance with the Rules of Procedure, and the means of evidence. The former consist of the written procedure, in the ad interim procedure, where the judge explores with the parties the possibility of a settlement, including through mediation and arbitration, using the facilities of the centre referred to in Article 35 and the oral procedure. The latter include, in particular, the hearing of the parties and the witnesses, the production of documents and sworn written statements (affidavits), experts opinions, requests for information, inspections, comparative tests or experiments. The procedure for taking such evidence is governed by the Rules of Procedure.

The Agreement specifies that, as a rule, the burden of proof of facts is on the party relying on those facts; however, when the subject matter of the patent is a process for obtaining a new product, any identical product produced without the consent of the patent owner, in the absence of proof to the contrary, is deemed to have been obtained by the patented process (Articles 52–55 of the Agreement).

v. Powers of the Court

These norms show the influence that the corresponding national provisions have exercised in the formulation of the measures, procedures and remedies that the Court may adopt and impose within the framework of the Agreement.

The Court may, by ordinance, order:

— the appointment of court experts in order to provide expertise for specific aspects of the case;
— the adoption of measures to protect confidential information in the course of the proceedings;
— the presentation of evidence;
— the adoption of effective provisional measures to preserve relevant evidence, including the inspection of premises;
— a party not to remove from its jurisdiction any assets located therein;
— the granting of an injunction against an alleged infringer intended to prevent any imminent infringement and against the infringer aimed at prohibiting the continuation of the infringement;
— the adoption of appropriate measures with regard to the infringing products and the materials used in the manufacture of the products, such as the destruction of the products and materials concerned;
— an infringer and third parties in possession of the infringing products or providing services in infringing activities to supply information as to the origin, quantities, price of the infringing products and identity of the individuals involved in the production and distribution of the products;
— the infringer to pay the injured party damages suffered as result of the infringement (Articles 57–64 and 67–68 of the Agreement).

The Court decides on the validity of a patent on the basis of an action of revocation or a counterclaim for revocation; it may revoke the patent either entirely or in part only on the grounds referred to in Articles 138(1) and 139(2) of the EPC. In actions concerning decisions of the EPO in relation to the carrying out of its tasks under Article 9 of Regulation (EU) 1257/2012, the Court may exercise any power entrusted to the EPO pursuant to the aforementioned article (Articles 65 and 66 of the Agreement).

vi. Appeals

An appeal may be brought before the Court of Appeal against a decision or an ordinance of the Court of First Instance by any party which has been unsuccessful, in whole or in part, in its submissions. An appeal against a decision or an order of the Court of First Instance may be based on points of law or matters of fact. Subject to exceptions and unless the Court decides otherwise upon the request of one of the parties, an appeal has no suspensive effect on the main proceedings (Articles 73 and 74 of the Agreement).

If the Court of Appeal decides that an appeal against a decision of the Court of First Instance is well-founded, it revokes the decision of the Court and gives a final decision. In exceptional cases provided for by the Rules of Procedure, the Court of Appeal may refer the case back to the Court of First Instance, which is bound by the decision of the Court of Appeal on points of law (Article 75 of the Agreement).

vii. Decisions

The provisions of the Agreement relating to the decisions and orders of the Court are also largely inspired by the corresponding norms in most national laws. These provisions deal with formal requirements of decisions and orders, which must be reasoned, in writing and in the language of proceedings, with the publication of the relevant text, at the request of the applicant and at the expense of the infringer, and with additional measures for the dissemination of information on the decision (Articles 77 and 80 of the Agreement).

A request for rehearing after a final decision of the Court may be exceptionally granted by the Court of Appeal upon the discovery of new decisive facts or in the event of a fundamental procedural defect (Article 81 of the Agreement).

Decisions and orders of the Court are enforceable in any contracting Member State. Without prejudice to the provisions of the Agreement and the Statute, enforcement procedures are governed by the law of the contracting Member Stat where the enforcement takes place (Article 81 of the Agreement).

C. Transitional Regime

The Agreement provides for the establishment of a transitional period of seven years after its date of entry into force. During this period, an action for infringement or revocation of a European patent or for a declaration of invalidity of a supplementary protection certificate for a product protected by a European patent can be still brought before competent national jurisdictions. The Agreement further provides that unless an action has already been initiated before the Court, the owner of a European patent granted or applied for prior to the end of the transitional period may opt out of the scope of application of the Agreement no later than one month before the expiry of the transitional period by a notification to the Registry and, unless an action has been brought before a national court, may withdraw the opt-out at any moment.

After five years following the entry into force of the Agreement, a broad consultation is carried out by the Administrative Committee with the users of the system and a survey in order to ascertain the number of actions for infringement or for revocation or a declaration of invalidity still pending before the national courts. On the basis of the result of this consultation, the Administrative Committee may prolong the transitional period by up to seven years (Article 83 of the Agreement).

8

The Implementation of the UPC Agreement

I. The Elements for the Entry into Force and for the Implementation of the UPC Agreement

It has already been noted that Article 89(1) of the UPC Agreement sets out the conditions for its entry into force. The first condition requires that the Agreement is ratified by 13 states, including France, Germany and the UK, while the second condition prescribes that the Agreement cannot enter into force prior to the entry into force of the amendments to Regulation (EU) 1215/2012 of 12 December 2012 on Jurisdiction and the Recognition and Enforcement of Judgments in Civil and Commercial Matters. The two conditions are substantially different, although they serve the same purpose. The first condition is self-explanatory; it reflects a common practice in international treaties in order to establish and guarantee a minimum level of consensus from the participating Member States concerning the implementation of the treaty provisions. The second condition makes the entry into force of the UPC Agreement dependent on a specific external element—the entry into force of the amended Regulation (EU) 1215/2012—which by the nature of its content is considered essential for the practical and successful implementation of the UPC Agreement. Besides these two conditions, by virtue of Article 89(1) of the UPC Agreement, there is a third element—the adoption of Rules of Procedure under the Agreement—that is expressly provided for under Article 41. Even if the Rules of Procedure are not listed as a condition for the entry into force of the Agreement, it is evident by their function that they are instrumental for its practical implementation after the entry into force.

In summary, it can be said that three elements play a role, respectively, to the entry into force of the UPC Agreement and to its practical implementation:

- ratification of the Agreement by the required minimum number of signatory states (Article 89(1));
- entry into force of the amended Regulation (EU) 1215/2012 (Article 89(1)); and
- adoption of the Rules of Procedure under the Agreement (Article 41).

Setting aside the question of the entry into force of the UPC Agreement by means of the required number of ratifications, which has already been dealt with, the present chapter concentrates on the recasting of Regulation (EU) 1215/2012 and on the adoption of the Rules of Procedure under the Agreement.

II. The Regime for the Allocation of Jurisdiction and for the Reciprocal Enforcement of Judgments

As already pointed out, the entry into force of the UPC Agreement is made dependent, inter alia, on the entry into force of the amendments to Regulation (EU) 1215/2012. In order to understand the reasons for this requirement, it is necessary to trace back and examine the structure of the existing regime for setting out a system for the allocation of jurisdiction and the reciprocal enforcement of judgments between the EU Member States, of which Regulation (EU) 1215/2012 constitutes the most recent expression.

This regime—the so-called 'Brussels Regime'—has undergone several changes since its establishment with the conclusion on 27 September 1968 of the Brussels Convention on Jurisdiction and the Enforcement of Judgments in Civil and Commercial Matters, which entered into force on 1 February 1973 between the six original EEC Member States (Belgium, France, Federal Republic of Germany, Italy, Luxembourg and the Netherlands). As was spelled out in its Preamble, the purpose of the Convention is to determine the international jurisdiction of the courts of the Member States, to facilitate recognition and to introduce an expeditious procedure for securing the enforcement of judgments, authentic instruments and court settlements. With a view to extending the regime set out by the Brussels Convention to the EFTA Member States, which were not eligible to become part of the Convention, a parallel treaty with virtually the same content, the Lugano Convention on Jurisdiction and the Enforcement of Judgments in Civil and Commercial Matters, was signed on 16 September 1988 between the EC and the EFTA Member States.

In order to develop measures relating to judicial cooperation in civil matters necessary for a sound operation of the Community internal market and in order that the relevant rules be governed by a Community legal instrument binding on and directly applicable to the Member States, on 22 December 2000 the EC Council adopted Regulation (EC) 44/2001 on jurisdiction and the recognition and enforcement of judgments in civil and commercial matters, which entered into force on 1 March 2002. The scope of the Regulation covers all main civil and commercial matters and for the purposes of the free movement of judgments, it ensures that judgments given in a Member State should be recognised and enforced in another Member State, even if the 'judgment debtor' is domiciled in a third state. Regulation (EC) 44/2001 (hereinafter the 'Brussels I Regulation') constitutes a substantial revision of the Brussels Convention.

In its turn, the Lugano Convention was revised by the Convention on Jurisdiction and the Recognition and Enforcement of Judgments in Civil and Commercial Matters. The revision took place at Lugano on 30 October 2007 between the EU and Denmark, Iceland, Norway and Switzerland.

On 21 April 2009, the Commission adopted a report on the application of Regulation (EC) 44/2001 concluding that, notwithstanding its satisfactory operation, it seemed desirable to improve the application of some of its provisions in order to further facilitate the free circulation of judgments and, in general, enhance access to justice. In the framework of the objective of the EU to establish an 'area of freedom, security and justice', new measures were to be adopted relating to judicial cooperation in civil matters, especially when differences between national rules governing jurisdiction and recognition of judgments risk hampering the free functioning of the internal market. These background considerations led to the revision of Regulation (EC) 44/2001 and to the adoption on 12 December 2012 of Regulation (EU) 1215/2012 on jurisdiction and the recognition and the enforcement of judgments in civil and commercial matters (hereinafter the 'Brussels I Regulation (recast)'), which became applicable on 10 January 2015, with the exception of Articles 75 and 76, which applied as of 10 January 2014.

III. The Brussels I Regulation (Recast)

The most significant changes introduced by the Brussels I Regulation (recast) may be summarised as follows:

— In order to avoid abusive litigation practices causing substantive delays in proceedings, the Regulation specifies that when a court other than the court designated in the 'choice of court agreement' is first seised and the designated court is subsequently seised in proceedings involving the same case and the same parties, the court that is first seised must hold its proceedings until the designated court rules on its jurisdiction.

— The Regulation clarifies that arbitration is excluded. When a court of a Member State is seised with a dispute involving arbitration, nothing should prevent that court from addressing the question of the validity of the arbitration agreement and referring the parties to arbitration.

— Further exceptions are provided for in the Regulation, under which a court of a Member State can exercise jurisdiction even when a defendant is not domiciled in the EU, eg, in matters relating to consumer contracts and to individual contracts of employment.

— Under the Regulation, the requirement of a declaration of enforceability (*exequatur*) is removed by abolishing the relevant process, so that a judgment given and enforceable in a Member State is enforceable in the other Member States without any declaration of enforceability being required.

At a regional level, the Brussels Regime is integrated by the provisions of the 31 March 1965 Treaty Concerning the Establishment and Statute of a Benelux Court of Justice (hereinafter 'the Benelux Court of Justice Agreement'). The Benelux Court of Justice is a jurisdiction common to the three Benelux countries and has the task of ensuring the application of rules common to the Benelux states, in particular in relation to trademarks, models and designs matters. On 15 October 2012, the three Benelux states signed a Protocol modifying the Agreement and creating the possibility of extending the jurisdictional competences of the Benelux Court of Justice to include specific matters which fall within the scope of the Brussels I Regulation (recast).

In practice, the coexistence of the instruments examined determines a triangular jurisdictional structure, whose three poles are constituted, respectively, by the UPC Agreement, the Brussels I Regulation (recast) and the Benelux Court of Justice Agreement. To ensure a combined and coherent application of these instruments and, at the same time, the entry into force of the UPC Agreement according to its Article 89(1), the EU Commission made a proposal on 26 July 2013 for a Regulation of the European Parliament and the Council amending Regulation (EU) 1215/2012 on jurisdiction and the recognition and enforcement of judgments in civil and commercial matters.[1] The following issues are addressed in this proposal:

- The UPC and the Benelux Court of Justice should be considered 'courts' within the meaning of the Brussels I Regulation (recast). This clarification is deemed necessary to ensure that the Regulation fully applies to these courts and that the international jurisdiction of the aforementioned courts is determined by the Regulation. Thus, defendants who would expect to be sued in a specific Member State by virtue of the provisions of the Regulation may be sued either before the UPC or the Benelux Court of Justice. This change of territorial jurisdiction needs to be clearly specified in the Regulation to enhance legal certainty for defendants.
- The Brussels I Regulation (recast) should prescribe how the provisions on jurisdiction of the Regulation should apply to the UPC and the Benelux Court of Justice, in the same manner as the existing Article 71 of the Regulation does for other international conventions on particular matters. To this end, a new paragraph 1 should be added into Article 71b, prescribing that the UPC and the Benelux Court of Justice should have jurisdiction at any time when a national court of the respective Member State would have jurisdiction on the basis of the provisions of the Regulation.
- In order to complete the jurisdictional rules of Brussels I Regulation (recast) insofar as defendants domiciled in a non-EU Member State are concerned, for matters which will fall within the competence of the UPC

[1] Commission, 'Proposal for a Regulation of the European Parliament and of the Council amending Regulation (EU) No 1215/2012 on jurisdiction and the recognition and enforcement of judgments in civil and commercial matters' COM (2013) 554 final.

and the Benelux Court of Justice, a new paragraph 2 should be added into Article 71b. It would extend the jurisdiction under the Regulation to disputes involving third state defendants domiciled in third states. As a result of this extension, access to the UPC and the Benelux Court of Justice is ensured in situations where the defendant is not domiciled in an EU Member State as access is ensured in situations where the defendant is domiciled in an EU Member State. Furthermore, a new paragraph 3 should be added into Article 71b proposing that a defendant not domiciled in an EU Member State can be sued before the UPC or the Benelux Court of Justice if: the property belonging to him is located in a Member State party to the Agreement establishing one of the two courts; the value of the property is not significant compared to the value of the claim; or the dispute has a sufficient connection with any Member State party to the Agreement establishing one of the two courts.

— A new Article 71c should provide that the provisions of Articles 29–32 of the Brussels I Regulation (recast) on lis pendens apply to proceedings before the UPC and the Benelux Court of Justice and before a court of a Member State not party to the Agreement establishing one of the two courts. Furthermore, the aforementioned provisions of the Brussels I Regulation (recast) should apply to proceedings before the UPC and before a court of a Member State party to the UPC Agreement during the transitional period referred to in Article 83(1) of the UPC Agreement.

— It is deemed important that the coherent and combined application of the provisions of the Brussels I Regulation (recast) and the UPC and the Benelux Court of Justice Agreements in matters of recognition and enforcement should be established. To this end, a new Article 71d should provide that the Regulation shall apply to the recognition and enforcement of judgments given by the UPC and the Benelux Court of Justice, which need to be recognised and enforced in Member States not party to the respective Agreements and judgments given by courts of Member States that are not parties to the respective Agreements which need to be recognised and enforced in Member States that are parties to the aforementioned Agreements.

The content of the Brussels I Regulation (recast), amended as summarised above by the EU Commission proposal of 26 July 2013, was endorsed by the EU Council on 4 March 2014 and applies as of 10 January 2015.

The revision process examined above concludes, for the time being, the series of modifications and adaptations to the Brussels Regime and establishes, in particular, the necessary operative links between the UPC Agreement and the Benelux Court of Justice Agreement necessary for the coherent functioning of the regime. Finally, it satisfies one of the conditions for the entry into force of the UPC Agreement, pending the deposit of the required number of ratifications.[2]

[2] On the Brussels I Regulation, see S Luginbuehl and D Stander, *Application of Revised Rules on Jurisdiction under I Regulation to Patent Lawsuits*, Journal of Intellectual Property Law & Practice, 2014.

IV. The Preparatory Committee for the Entry into Force of the UPC Agreement and the Rules of Procedure

Following the adoption of the UPC, the Preparatory Committee of the UPC was set up in March 2013 by the 25 Member States that signed the UPC Agreement on 19 February 2013. The Commission and the EPO have observer status. The institutional task of the Committee is to deal with the necessary preparations for the coming into force of the Agreement. The Committee's work is conducted on the basis of a so-called 'road map'. According to the basic principles of this outline, the first aim is the date of the entry into force of the UPC, which was tentatively fixed for early 2015. In order for the UPC to be fully operational on the set date, it is necessary that the Committee establishes a scenario providing for a transition from the preparatory stage to the operational stage. To this end, the Committee's activities are organised into five working areas.

— legal framework;
— financial aspects;
— IT system;
— facilities;
— human resources and training.

Financial regulations are to be prepared regarding the establishment, structure and implementation of the budget. The Preparatory Committee has the task of developing an electronic filing and case management system (IT system), including public online inspection of certain parts of the files and the development of a court website. The signatory states hosting a local, regional or central division of the Court of First Instance or the Court of Appeal indicated that they are prepared to have the appropriate facilities in term of premises in place before the entry into force of the Agreement. Preparations are made for the organisation of the training of candidate judges, the nomination of the first group of judges and the organisation of the initial pool of judges.

The task of preparing Rules of Procedure under the UPC Agreement has been allocated to the legal framework working area. In this respect, it should be recalled once again that Article 41 of the UPC Agreement expressly provides for the adoption of Rules of Procedure by the Administrative Committee on the basis of broad consultations and following the opinion of the Commission as to the compatibility of the Rules with EU law. This set of provisions should complement the basic principles of procedural law already contained in Part III of the Agreement. Within these provisions, specific references are made to procedural details to be spelled out in the Rules, in particular those relating to proceedings before the Court, powers of the Court, appeals and decisions.

An Expert Group, composed of practitioners, is in charge of drafting the Rules of Procedure, which are subject to a broad consultation with professional and industry bodies in order that these norms guarantee the uniform application of the decisions of the Court and that proceedings are structured in the most efficient manner. At present, 16 drafts of the Rules of Procedure have been prepared and discussed. The sixteenth draft is composed of 382 rules, which are grouped in five parts, providing specific procedural details corresponding to the different stages of the procedures before the Court of First Instance, such as means of evidence and of obtaining evidence and provisional measures, procedures before the Court of Appeal and general procedural provisions applicable in proceedings before the Court.

It derives from what has been indicated above that, in general, the work of the Preparatory Committee and, in particular, of the Expert Group in preparing the Rules of Procedure is far from being completed; thus, the operations for the entry into force of the UPC Agreement are still to be regarded as a 'work in progress'.

Conclusion

It has already been pointed out that the creation of a unitary patent system for the protection of inventions within the EU resulted from the adoption by the European Parliament on 11 December 2012 of three acts of different legal natures: two Regulations on the creation of the unitary system and an international agreement on the setting up of a unified jurisdiction for patent disputes. In this context, the two Regulations should be considered the 'engine' of the unitary system because of their direct applicability in the legal systems of the Member States, thus guaranteeing its actual applicability. The international agreement which, in essence, supersedes and synthesises the corresponding functions of national patent courts represents the decision of the contracting Member States to delegate these functions to a supranational institution as a necessary complement for the practical functioning of the unitary patent protection system. The interaction of the three acts provides the users of the patent system, on the one hand, with a legal title for the protection of inventions—the European patent with unitary effect—common to the EU Member States and, on the other hand, the owners of this title with the advantages of a unified jurisdiction for the defence of their patent rights.

In this connection, it seems important to note that the adoption of a Regulation for the creation and functioning of the unitary patent protection system and of an international treaty with the task of setting up and regulating a unified patent jurisdiction has avoided a blocking situation similar to that which in 1989 resulted in the definitive non-entry into force of the CPC, whose intent was to encompass the Community patent system in the framework of a single international instrument.

A new legal structure which intends to regulate a complex area, such as that of a unitary patent system, at a regional level needs, by definition, the necessary time to prove its capability to work in conformity with its features and intended scope. This is particularly true in the case of an international instrument like the UPC Agreement, which aims to set out common provisions applicable to a sensitive legal domain for any contracting Member State such as that of jurisdiction. In this case, only the daily application of the mechanisms of the Agreement may show the efficacy and functionality of the agreed norms. These peculiarities were clear in the mind of the authors of the Agreement and they are reflected in the provisions of Article 83 on the transitional period and, to a large extent, in those of Article 87, which foresee detailed modalities for the revision of the text of the Agreement, subject to consultations with the users of the patent system on the functioning, efficiency and cost-effectiveness of the Court and the quality of the Court's decisions.

These last considerations above are not intended to diminish in any way the scope and meaning of the results of the harmonisation efforts that more than a decade of complex negotiations have offered to the Member States of the EU and to the entire international community. On the contrary, they should be read as an expression of unconditional praise for a rare case of the success of intergovernmental cooperation and for the establishment of a precedent which will condition any future project relating to the harmonisation of national provisions in fields other than that of industrial property.

APPENDICES

I. Regulation (EU) No 1257/2012 of the European Parliament and of the Council of 17 December 2012 implementing enhanced cooperation in the area of the creation of unitary patent protection

II. Regulation (EU) No 1260/2012 of the Council of 17 December 2012 implementing enhanced cooperation in the area of the creation of unitary patent protection with regard to the applicable translation arrangements

III. Agreement on a Unified Patent Court and Statute of the Unified Patent Court

I.

REGULATION (EU) NO 1257/2012 OF THE EUROPEAN PARLIAMENT AND OF THE COUNCIL

of 17 December 2012

implementing enhanced cooperation in the area of the creation of unitary patent protection

THE EUROPEAN PARLIAMENT AND THE COUNCIL OF THE EUROPEAN UNION,

Having regard to the Treaty on the Functioning of the European Union and in particular the first paragraph of Article 118 thereof,

Having regard to Council Decision 2011/167/EU of 10 March 2011 authorising enhanced cooperation in the area of the creation of unitary patent protection (1),

Having regard to the proposal from the European Commission,

After transmission of the draft legislative act to the national parliaments,

Acting in accordance with the ordinary legislative procedure (2),

Whereas:

(1) The creation of the legal conditions enabling undertakings to adapt their activities in manufacturing and distributing products across national borders and providing them with greater choice and more opportunities contributes to the attainment of the objectives of the Union set out in Article 3(3) of the Treaty on European Union. Uniform patent protection within the internal market, or at least a significant part thereof, should feature amongst the legal instruments which undertakings have at their disposal.

(2) Pursuant to the first paragraph of Article 118 of the Treaty on the Functioning of the European Union (TFEU), measures to be taken in the context of the establishment and functioning of the internal market include the creation of uniform patent protection throughout the Union and the establishment of centralised Union-wide authorisation, coordination and supervision arrangements.

(3) On 10 March 2011, the Council adopted Decision 2011/167/EU authorising enhanced cooperation between Belgium, Bulgaria, the Czech Republic, Denmark, Germany, Estonia, Ireland, Greece, France, Cyprus, Latvia, Lithuania, Luxembourg, Hungary, Malta, the Netherlands, Austria, Poland, Portugal, Romania, Slovenia, Slovakia, Finland, Sweden and the United Kingdom (hereinafter 'participating Member States') in the area of the creation of unitary patent protection.

(4) Unitary patent protection will foster scientific and technological advances and the functioning of the internal market by making access to the patent system easier, less costly and legally secure. It will also improve the level of patent protection by making it possible to obtain uniform patent protection

in the participating Member States and eliminate costs and complexity for undertakings throughout the Union. It should be available to proprietors of a European patent from both the participating Member States and from other States, regardless of their nationality, residence or place of establishment.

(5) The Convention on the Grant of European Patents of 5 October 1973, as revised on 17 December 1991 and on 29 November 2000 (hereinafter 'EPC'), established the European Patent Organisation and entrusted it with the task of granting European patents. This task is carried out by the European Patent Office (hereinafter 'EPO'). A European patent granted by the EPO should, at the request of the patent proprietor, benefit from unitary effect by virtue of this Regulation in the participating Member States. Such a patent is hereinafter referred to as a 'European patent with unitary effect'.

(6) In accordance with Part IX of the EPC a group of Contracting States to the EPC may provide that European patents granted for those States have a unitary character. This Regulation constitutes a special agreement within the meaning of Article 142 of the EPC, a regional patent treaty within the meaning of Article 45(1) of the Patent Cooperation Treaty of 19 June 1970 as last modified on 3 February 2001 and a special agreement within the meaning of Article 19 of the Convention for the Protection of Industrial Property, signed in Paris on 20 March 1883 and last amended on 28 September 1979.

(7) Unitary patent protection should be achieved by attributing unitary effect to European patents in the post-grant phase by virtue of this Regulation and in respect of all the participating Member States. The main feature of a European patent with unitary effect should be its unitary character, i.e. providing uniform protection and having equal effect in all the participating Member States. Consequently, a European patent with unitary effect should only be limited, transferred or revoked, or lapse, in respect of all the participating Member States. It should be possible for a European patent with unitary effect to be licensed in respect of the whole or part of the territories of the participating Member States. To ensure the uniform substantive scope of protection conferred by unitary patent protection, only European patents that have been granted for all the participating Member States with the same set of claims should benefit from unitary effect. Finally, the unitary effect attributed to a European patent should have an accessory nature and should be deemed not to have arisen to the extent that the basic European patent has been revoked or limited.

(8) In accordance with the general principles of patent law and Article 64(1) of the EPC, unitary patent protection should take effect retroactively in the participating Member States as from the date of publication of the mention of the grant of the European patent in the European Patent Bulletin. Where unitary patent protection takes effect, the participating Member States should ensure that the European patent is deemed not to have taken effect on their territory as a national patent, so as to avoid any duplication of patent protection.

(9) The European patent with unitary effect should confer on its proprietor the right to prevent any third party from committing acts against which the patent provides protection. This should be ensured through the establishment of a Unified Patent Court. In matters not covered by this Regulation or by Council Regulation (EU) No 1260/2012 of 17 December 2012 implementing enhanced cooperation in the area of unitary patent protection with regard to the applicable translation arrangements (3), the provisions of the EPC, the Agreement on a Unified Patent Court, including its provisions defining the scope of that right and its limitations, and national law, including rules of private international law, should apply.

(10) Compulsory licences for European patents with unitary effect should be governed by the laws of the participating Member States as regards their respective territories.

(11) In its report on the operation of this Regulation, the Commission should evaluate the functioning of the applicable limitations and, where necessary, make appropriate proposals, taking account of the contribution of the patent system to innovation and technological progress, the legitimate interests of third parties and overriding interests of society. The Agreement on a Unified Patent Court does not preclude the European Union from exercising its powers in this field.

(12) In accordance with the case-law of the Court of Justice of the European Union, the principle of the exhaustion of rights should also be applied to European patents with unitary effect. Therefore, rights conferred by a European patent with unitary effect should not extend to acts concerning the product covered by that patent which are carried out within the participating Member States after that product has been placed on the market in the Union by the patent proprietor.

(13) The regime applicable to damages should be governed by the laws of the participating Member States, in particular the provisions implementing Article 13 of Directive 2004/48/EC of the European Parliament and of the Council of 29 April 2004 on the enforcement of intellectual property rights (4).

(14) As an object of property, a European patent with unitary effect should be dealt with in its entirety, and in all the participating Member States, as a national patent of the participating Member State determined in accordance with specific criteria such as the applicant's residence, principal place of business or place of business.

(15) In order to promote and facilitate the economic exploitation of an invention protected by a European patent with unitary effect, the proprietor of that patent should be able to offer it to be licensed in return for appropriate consideration. To that end, the patent proprietor should be able to file a statement with the EPO that he is prepared to grant a license in return for appropriate consideration. In that case, the patent proprietor should benefit from a reduction of the renewal fees as from the EPO's receipt of such statement.

(16) The group of Member States making use of the provisions of Part IX of the EPC may give tasks to the EPO and set up a select committee of the Administrative Council of the European Patent Organisation (hereinafter 'Select Committee').

(17) The participating Member States should give certain administrative tasks relating to European patents with unitary effect to the EPO, in particular as regards the administration of requests for unitary effect, the registration of unitary effect and of any limitation, licence, transfer, revocation or lapse of European patents with unitary effect, the collection and distribution of renewal fees, the publication of translations for information purposes during a transitional period and the administration of a compensation scheme for the reimbursement of translation costs incurred by applicants filing European patent applications in a language other than one of the official languages of the EPO.

(18) In the framework of the Select Committee, the participating Member States should ensure the governance and supervision of the activities related to the tasks entrusted to the EPO by the participating Member States, ensure that requests for unitary effect are filed with the EPO within one month of the date of publication of the mention of the grant in the European Patent Bulletin and ensure that such requests are submitted in the language of the proceedings before the EPO together with the translation prescribed, during a transitional period, by Regulation (EU) No 1260/2012. The participating Member States should also ensure the setting, in accordance with the voting rules laid down in Article 35(2) of the EPC, of the level of the renewal fees and the share of the distribution of the renewal fees in accordance with the criteria set out in this Regulation.

(19) Patent proprietors should pay a single annual renewal fee for a European patent with unitary effect. Renewal fees should be progressive throughout the term of the patent protection and, together with the fees to be paid to the European Patent Organisation during the pre-grant stage, should cover all costs associated with the grant of the European patent and the administration of the unitary patent protection. The level of the renewal fees should be set with the aim of facilitating innovation and fostering the competitiveness of European businesses, taking into account the situation of specific entities such as small and medium-sized enterprises, for example in the form of lower fees. It should also reflect the size of the market covered by the patent and be similar to the level of the national renewal fees for an average European patent taking effect in the participating Member States at the time when the level of the renewal fees is first set.

(20) The appropriate level and distribution of renewal fees should be determined in order to ensure that, in relation to the unitary patent protection, all costs of the tasks entrusted to the EPO are fully covered by the resources generated by the European patents with unitary effect and that, together with the fees to be paid to the European Patent Organisation during the

pre-grant stage, the revenues from the renewal fees ensure a balanced budget of the European Patent Organisation.

(21) Renewal fees should be paid to the European Patent Organisation. The EPO should retain an amount to cover the expenses generated at the EPO in carrying out tasks in relation to the unitary patent protection in accordance with Article 146 of the EPC. The remaining amount should be distributed among the participating Member States and should be used for patent-related purposes. The share of distribution should be set on the basis of fair, equitable and relevant criteria, namely the level of patent activity and the size of the market, and should guarantee a minimum amount to be distributed to each participating Member State in order to maintain a balanced and sustainable functioning of the system. The distribution should provide compensation for having an official language other than one of the official languages of the EPO, having a disproportionately low level of patenting activity established on the basis of the European Innovation Scoreboard, and/or having acquired membership of the European Patent Organisation relatively recently.

(22) An enhanced partnership between the EPO and central industrial property offices of the Member States should enable the EPO to make regular use, where appropriate, of the result of any search carried out by central industrial property offices on a national patent application the priority of which is claimed in a subsequent European patent application. All central industrial property offices, including those which do not perform searches in the course of a national patent-granting procedure, can play an essential role under the enhanced partnership, inter alia, by giving advice and support to potential patent applicants, in particular small and medium-sized enterprises, by receiving applications, by forwarding applications to the EPO and by disseminating patent information.

(23) This Regulation is complemented by Regulation (EU) No 1260/2012, adopted by the Council in accordance with the second paragraph of Article 118 of the TFEU.

(24) Jurisdiction in respect of European patents with unitary effect should be established and governed by an instrument setting up a unified patent litigation system for European patents and European patents with unitary effect.

(25) Establishing a Unified Patent Court to hear cases concerning the European patent with unitary effect is essential in order to ensure the proper functioning of that patent, consistency of case-law and hence legal certainty, and cost-effectiveness for patent proprietors. It is therefore of paramount importance that the participating Member States ratify the Agreement on a Unified Patent Court in accordance with their national constitutional and parliamentary procedures and take the necessary steps for that Court to become operational as soon as possible.

(26) This Regulation should be without prejudice to the right of the participating Member States to grant national patents and should not replace the participating Member States' laws on patents. Patent applicants should remain free to obtain either a national patent, a European patent with unitary effect, a European patent taking effect in one or more of the Contracting States to the EPC or a European patent with unitary effect validated in addition in one or more other Contracting States to the EPC which are not among the participating Member States.

(27) Since the objective of this Regulation, namely the creation of unitary patent protection, cannot be sufficiently achieved by the Member States and can therefore, by reason of the scale and effects of this Regulation, be better achieved at Union level, the Union may adopt measures, where appropriate by means of enhanced cooperation, in accordance with the principle of subsidiarity as set out in Article 5 of the Treaty on European Union. In accordance with the principle of proportionality, as set out in that Article, this Regulation does not go beyond what is necessary in order to achieve that objective,

HAVE ADOPTED THIS REGULATION:
CHAPTER I

GENERAL PROVISIONS

Article 1
Subject matter

1. This Regulation implements enhanced cooperation in the area of the creation of unitary patent protection, authorised by Decision 2011/167/EU.
2. This Regulation constitutes a special agreement within the meaning of Article 142 of the Convention on the Grant of European Patents of 5 October 1973, as revised on 17 December 1991 and on 29 November 2000 (hereinafter 'EPC').

Article 2
Definitions

For the purposes of this Regulation, the following definitions shall apply:

(a) 'Participating Member State' means a Member State which participates in enhanced cooperation in the area of the creation of unitary patent protection by virtue of Decision 2011/167/EU, or by virtue of a decision adopted in accordance with the second or third subparagraph of Article 331(1) of the TFEU, at the time the request for unitary effect as referred to in Article 9 is made;

(b) 'European patent' means a patent granted by the European Patent Office (hereinafter 'EPO') under the rules and procedures laid down in the EPC;
(c) 'European patent with unitary effect' means a European patent which benefits from unitary effect in the participating Member States by virtue of this Regulation;
(d) 'European Patent Register' means the register kept by the EPO under Article 127 of the EPC;
(e) 'Register for unitary patent protection' means the register constituting part of the European Patent Register in which the unitary effect and any limitation, licence, transfer, revocation or lapse of a European patent with unitary effect are registered;
(f) 'European Patent Bulletin' means the periodical publication provided for in Article 129 of the EPC.

Article 3
European patent with unitary effect

1. A European patent granted with the same set of claims in respect of all the participating Member States shall benefit from unitary effect in the participating Member States provided that its unitary effect has been registered in the Register for unitary patent protection.
   A European patent granted with different sets of claims for different participating Member States shall not benefit from unitary effect.
2. A European patent with unitary effect shall have a unitary character. It shall provide uniform protection and shall have equal effect in all the participating Member States.
   It may only be limited, transferred or revoked, or lapse, in respect of all the participating Member States.
   It may be licensed in respect of the whole or part of the territories of the participating Member States.
3. The unitary effect of a European patent shall be deemed not to have arisen to the extent that the European patent has been revoked or limited.

Article 4
Date of effect

1. A European patent with unitary effect shall take effect in the participating Member States on the date of publication by the EPO of the mention of the grant of the European patent in the European Patent Bulletin.
2. The participating Member States shall take the necessary measures to ensure that, where the unitary effect of a European patent has been registered and extends to their territory, that European patent is deemed not to have taken effect as a national patent in their territory on the date of publication of the mention of the grant in the European Patent Bulletin.

CHAPTER II

EFFECTS OF A EUROPEAN PATENT WITH UNITARY EFFECT

Article 5
Uniform protection

1. The European patent with unitary effect shall confer on its proprietor the right to prevent any third party from committing acts against which that patent provides protection throughout the territories of the participating Member States in which it has unitary effect, subject to applicable limitations.
2. The scope of that right and its limitations shall be uniform in all participating Member States in which the patent has unitary effect.
3. The acts against which the patent provides protection referred to in paragraph 1 and the applicable limitations shall be those defined by the law applied to European patents with unitary effect in the participating Member State whose national law is applicable to the European patent with unitary effect as an object of property in accordance with Article 7.
4. In its report referred to in Article 16(1), the Commission shall evaluate the functioning of the applicable limitations and shall, where necessary, make appropriate proposals.

Article 6
Exhaustion of the rights conferred by a European patent with unitary effect

The rights conferred by a European patent with unitary effect shall not extend to acts concerning a product covered by that patent which are carried out within the participating Member States in which that patent has unitary effect after that product has been placed on the market in the Union by, or with the consent of, the patent proprietor, unless there are legitimate grounds for the patent proprietor to oppose further commercialisation of the product.

CHAPTER III

A EUROPEAN PATENT WITH UNITARY EFFECT AS AN OBJECT OF PROPERTY

Article 7
Treating a European patent with unitary effect as a national patent

1. A European patent with unitary effect as an object of property shall be treated in its entirety and in all the participating Member States as a national patent of the participating Member State in which that patent has unitary effect and in which, according to the European Patent Register:
   (a) the applicant had his residence or principal place of business on the date of filing of the application for the European patent; or

(b) where point (a) does not apply, the applicant had a place of business on the date of filing of the application for the European patent.

2. Where two or more persons are entered in the European Patent Register as joint applicants, point (a) of paragraph 1 shall apply to the joint applicant indicated first. Where this is not possible, point (a) of paragraph 1 shall apply to the next joint applicant indicated in the order of entry. Where point (a) of paragraph 1 does not apply to any of the joint applicants, point (b) of paragraph 1 shall apply accordingly.
3. Where no applicant had his residence, principal place of business or place of business in a participating Member State in which that patent has unitary effect for the purposes of paragraphs 1 or 2, the European patent with unitary effect as an object of property shall be treated in its entirety and in all the participating Member States as a national patent of the State where the European Patent Organisation has its headquarters in accordance with Article 6(1) of the EPC.
4. The acquisition of a right may not be dependent on any entry in a national patent register.

Article 8
Licences of right

1. The proprietor of a European patent with unitary effect may file a statement with the EPO to the effect that the proprietor is prepared to allow any person to use the invention as a licensee in return for appropriate consideration.
2. A licence obtained under this Regulation shall be treated as a contractual licence.

CHAPTER IV

INSTITUTIONAL PROVISIONS

Article 9
Administrative tasks in the framework of the European Patent Organisation

1. The participating Member States shall, within the meaning of Article 143 of the EPC, give the EPO the following tasks, to be carried out in accordance with the internal rules of the EPO:
   (a) to administer requests for unitary effect by proprietors of European patents;
   (b) to include the Register for unitary patent protection within the European Patent Register and to administer the Register for unitary patent protection;
   (c) to receive and register statements on licensing referred to in Article 8, their withdrawal and licensing commitments undertaken by the proprietor of the European patent with unitary effect in international standardisation bodies;

(d) to publish the translations referred to in Article 6 of Regulation (EU) No 1260/2012 during the transitional period referred to in that Article;
(e) to collect and administer renewal fees for European patents with unitary effect, in respect of the years following the year in which the mention of the grant is published in the European Patent Bulletin; to collect and administer additional fees for late payment of renewal fees where such late payment is made within six months of the due date, as well as to distribute part of the collected renewal fees to the participating Member States;
(f) to administer the compensation scheme for the reimbursement of translation costs referred to in Article 5 of Regulation (EU) No 1260/2012;
(g) to ensure that a request for unitary effect by a proprietor of a European patent is submitted in the language of the proceedings as defined in Article 14(3) of the EPC no later than one month after the mention of the grant is published in the European Patent Bulletin; and
(h) to ensure that the unitary effect is indicated in the Register for unitary patent protection, where a request for unitary effect has been filed and, during the transitional period provided for in Article 6 of Regulation (EU) No 1260/2012, has been submitted together with the translations referred to in that Article, and that the EPO is informed of any limitations, licences, transfers or revocations of European patents with unitary effect.

2. The participating Member States shall ensure compliance with this Regulation in fulfilling their international obligations undertaken in the EPC and shall cooperate to that end. In their capacity as Contracting States to the EPC, the participating Member States shall ensure the governance and supervision of the activities related to the tasks referred to in paragraph 1 of this Article and shall ensure the setting of the level of renewal fees in accordance with Article 12 of this Regulation and the setting of the share of distribution of the renewal fees in accordance with Article 13 of this Regulation.
To that end they shall set up a select committee of the Administrative Council of the European Patent Organisation (hereinafter 'Select Committee') within the meaning of Article 145 of the EPC.
The Select Committee shall consist of the representatives of the participating Member States and a representative of the Commission as an observer, as well as alternates who will represent them in their absence. The members of the Select Committee may be assisted by advisers or experts.
Decisions of the Select Committee shall be taken with due regard for the position of the Commission and in accordance with the rules laid down in Article 35(2) of the EPC.
3. The participating Member States shall ensure effective legal protection before a competent court of one or several participating Member States against the decisions of the EPO in carrying out the tasks referred to in paragraph 1.

CHAPTER V

FINANCIAL PROVISIONS

Article 10
Principle on expenses

The expenses incurred by the EPO in carrying out the additional tasks given to it, within the meaning of Article 143 of the EPC, by the participating Member States shall be covered by the fees generated by the European patents with unitary effect.

Article 11
Renewal fees

1. Renewal fees for European patents with unitary effect and additional fees for their late payment shall be paid to the European Patent Organisation by the patent proprietor. Those fees shall be due in respect of the years following the year in which the mention of the grant of the European patent which benefits from unitary effect is published in the European Patent Bulletin.
2. A European patent with unitary effect shall lapse if a renewal fee and, where applicable, any additional fee have not been paid in due time.
3. Renewal fees which fall due after receipt of the statement referred to in Article 8(1) shall be reduced.

Article 12
Level of renewal fees

1. Renewal fees for European patents with unitary effect shall be:
   (a) progressive throughout the term of the unitary patent protection;
   (b) sufficient to cover all costs associated with the grant of the European patent and the administration of the unitary patent protection; and
   (c) sufficient, together with the fees to be paid to the European Patent Organisation during the pre-grant stage, to ensure a balanced budget of the European Patent Organisation.
2. The level of the renewal fees shall be set, taking into account, among others, the situation of specific entities such as small and medium-sized enterprises, with the aim of:
   (a) facilitating innovation and fostering the competitiveness of European businesses;
   (b) reflecting the size of the market covered by the patent; and
   (c) being similar to the level of the national renewal fees for an average European patent taking effect in the participating Member States at the time the level of the renewal fees is first set.
3. In order to attain the objectives set out in this Chapter, the level of renewal fees shall be set at a level that:
   (a) is equivalent to the level of the renewal fee to be paid for the average geographical coverage of current European patents;

(b) reflects the renewal rate of current European patents; and
(c) reflects the number of requests for unitary effect.

Article 13
Distribution

1. The EPO shall retain 50 per cent of the renewal fees referred to in Article 11 paid for European patents with unitary effect. The remaining amount shall be distributed to the participating Member States in accordance with the share of distribution of the renewal fees set pursuant to Article 9(2).
2. In order to attain the objectives set out in this Chapter, the share of distribution of renewal fees among the participating Member States shall be based on the following fair, equitable and relevant criteria:

   (a) the number of patent applications;
   (b) the size of the market, while ensuring a minimum amount to be distributed to each participating Member State;
   (c) compensation to the participating Member States which have:
      (i) an official language other than one of the official languages of the EPO;
      (ii) a disproportionately low level of patenting activity; and/or
      (iii) acquired membership of the European Patent Organisation relatively recently.

CHAPTER VI

FINAL PROVISIONS

Article 14
Cooperation between the Commission and the EPO

The Commission shall establish a close cooperation through a working agreement with the EPO in the fields covered by this Regulation. This cooperation shall include regular exchanges of views on the functioning of the working agreement and, in particular, on the issue of renewal fees and their impact on the budget of the European Patent Organisation.

Article 15
Application of competition law and the law relating to unfair competition

This Regulation shall be without prejudice to the application of competition law and the law relating to unfair competition.

Article 16
Report on the operation of this Regulation

1. Not later than three years from the date on which the first European patent with unitary effect takes effect, and every five years thereafter, the

Commission shall present to the European Parliament and the Council a report on the operation of this Regulation and, where necessary, make appropriate proposals for amending it.

2. The Commission shall regularly submit to the European Parliament and the Council reports on the functioning of the renewal fees referred to in Article 11, with particular emphasis on compliance with Article 12.

Article 17
Notification by the participating Member States

1. The participating Member States shall notify the Commission of the measures adopted in accordance with Article 9 by the date of application of this Regulation.
2. Each participating Member State shall notify the Commission of the measures adopted in accordance with Article 4(2) by the date of application of this Regulation or, in the case of a participating Member State in which the Unified Patent Court does not have exclusive jurisdiction with regard to European patents with unitary effect on the date of application of this Regulation, by the date from which the Unified Patent Court has such exclusive jurisdiction in that participating Member State.

Article 18
Entry into force and application

1. This Regulation shall enter into force on the twentieth day following that of its publication in the Official Journal of the European Union.
2. It shall apply from 1 January 2014 or the date of entry into force of the Agreement on a Unified Patent Court (the 'Agreement'), whichever is the later.

   By way of derogation from Articles 3(1), 3(2) and 4(1), a European patent for which unitary effect is registered in the Register for unitary patent protection shall have unitary effect only in those participating Member States in which the Unified Patent Court has exclusive jurisdiction with regard to European patents with unitary effect at the date of registration.
3. Each participating Member State shall notify the Commission of its ratification of the Agreement at the time of deposit of its ratification instrument. The Commission shall publish in the Official Journal of the European Union the date of entry into force of the Agreement and a list of the Member States who have ratified the Agreement at the date of entry into force. The Commission shall thereafter regularly update the list of the participating Member States which have ratified the Agreement and shall publish such updated list in the Official Journal of the European Union.
4. The participating Member States shall ensure that the measures referred to in Article 9 are in place by the date of application of this Regulation.
5. Each participating Member State shall ensure that the measures referred to in Article 4(2) are in place by the date of application of this Regulation or, in the case of a participating Member State in which the Unified Patent Court does not have exclusive jurisdiction with regard to European patents with unitary

effect on the date of application of this Regulation, by the date from which the Unified Patent Court has such exclusive jurisdiction in that participating Member State.

6. Unitary patent protection may be requested for any European patent granted on or after the date of application of this Regulation.

This Regulation shall be binding in its entirety and directly applicable in the participating Member States in accordance with the Treaties.

Done at Brussels, 17 December 2012.

For the European Parliament
The President
M. SCHULZ

For the Council
The President
A. D. MAVROYIANNIS

(1) OJ L76, 22.3.2011, p. 53.
(2) Position of the European Parliament of 11 December 2012 (not yet published in the Official Journal) and decision of the Council of 17 December 2012.
(3) See page 89 of this Official Journal.
(4) OJ L157, 30.4.2004, p. 45.

II.

COUNCIL REGULATION (EU) No 1260/2012

of 17 December 2012

implementing enhanced cooperation in the area of the creation of unitary patent protection with regard to the applicable translation arrangements

THE COUNCIL OF THE EUROPEAN UNION,

Having regard to the Treaty on the Functioning of the European Union, and in particular the second paragraph of Article 118 thereof,

Having regard to Council Decision 2011/167/EU of 10 March 2011 authorising enhanced cooperation in the area of the creation of unitary patent protection (1),

Having regard to the proposal from the European Commission,

After transmission of the draft legislative act to the national parliaments,

Having regard to the opinion of the European Parliament,

Acting in accordance with a special legislative procedure,

Whereas:

(1) Pursuant to Decision 2011/167/EU, Belgium, Bulgaria, the Czech Republic, Denmark, Germany, Estonia, Ireland, Greece, France, Cyprus, Latvia, Lithuania, Luxembourg, Hungary, Malta, the Netherlands, Austria, Poland, Portugal, Romania, Slovenia, Slovakia, Finland, Sweden and the United Kingdom (hereinafter 'participating Member States') were authorised to establish enhanced cooperation between themselves in the area of the creation of unitary patent protection.

(2) Under Regulation (EU) No 1257/2012 of the European Parliament and of the Council of 17 December 2012 implementing enhanced cooperation in the area of the creation of unitary patent protection (2), certain European patents granted by the European Patent Office (hereinafter 'EPO') under the rules and procedures of the Convention on the Grant of European Patents of 5 October 1973, as revised on 17 December 1991 and on 29 November 2000 (hereinafter 'EPC') should, at the request of the patent proprietor, benefit from unitary effect in the participating Member States.

(3) Translation arrangements for European patents benefiting from unitary effect in the participating Member States (hereinafter 'European patent with unitary effect') should be established by means of a separate Regulation, in accordance with the second paragraph of Article 118 of the Treaty on the Functioning of the European Union (TFEU).

(4) In accordance with Decision 2011/167/EU the translation arrangements for European patents with unitary effect should be simple and cost-effective. They should correspond to those provided for in the proposal for a Council Regulation on the translation arrangements for the European Union patent, presented by the Commission on 30 June 2010, combined with the elements of compromise proposed by the Presidency in November 2010 that had wide support in the Council.

(5) Such translation arrangements should ensure legal certainty and stimulate innovation and should, in particular, benefit small and medium-sized enterprises (SMEs). They should make access to the European patent with unitary effect and to the patent system as a whole easier, less costly and legally secure.

(6) Since the EPO is responsible for the grant of European patents, the translation arrangements for the European patent with unitary effect should be built on the current procedure in the EPO. Those arrangements should aim to achieve the necessary balance between the interests of economic operators and the public interest, in terms of the cost of proceedings and the availability of technical information.

(7) Without prejudice to the transitional arrangements, where the specification of a European patent with unitary effect has been published in accordance with Article 14(6) of the EPC, no further translations should be required. Article 14(6) of the EPC provides that the specification of a European patent is published in the language of the proceedings before the EPO and includes a translation of the claims into the other two official languages of the EPO.

(8) In the event of a dispute concerning a European patent with unitary effect, it is a legitimate requirement that the patent proprietor at the request of the alleged infringer should provide a full translation of the patent into an official language of either the participating Member State in which the alleged infringement took place or the Member State in which the alleged infringer is domiciled. The patent proprietor should also be required to provide, at the request of a court competent in the participating Member States for disputes concerning the European patent with unitary effect, a full translation of the patent into the language used in the proceedings of that court. Such translations should not be carried out by automated means and should be provided at the expense of the patent proprietor.

(9) In the event of a dispute concerning a claim for damages, the court hearing the dispute should take into consideration the fact that, before having been provided with a translation in his own language, the alleged infringer may have acted in good faith and may have not known or had reasonable grounds to know that he was infringing the patent. The competent court should assess the circumstances of the individual case and, inter alia, should take into account whether the alleged infringer is a SME operating only at local level, the language of the proceedings before the EPO and, during the transitional period, the translation submitted together with the request for unitary effect.

(10) In order to facilitate access to European patents with unitary effect, in particular for SMEs, applicants should be able to file their patent applications at the EPO in any official language of the Union. As a complementary measure, certain applicants obtaining European patents with unitary effect, having filed a European patent application in one of the official languages of the Union, which is not an official language of the EPO, and having their

residence or principal place of business within a Member State, should receive additional reimbursements of the costs of translating from the language of the patent application into the language of the proceedings of the EPO, beyond what is currently in place at the EPO. Such reimbursements should be administered by the EPO in accordance with Article 9 of Regulation (EU) No 1257/2012.

(11) In order to promote the availability of patent information and the dissemination of technological knowledge, machine translations of patent applications and specifications into all official languages of the Union should be available as soon as possible. Machine translations are being developed by the EPO and are a very important tool in seeking to improve access to patent information and to widely disseminate technological knowledge. The timely availability of high quality machine translations of European patent applications and specifications into all official languages of the Union would benefit all users of the European patent system. Machine translations are a key feature of European Union policy. Such machine translations should serve for information purposes only and should not have any legal effect.

(12) During the transitional period, before a system of high quality machine translations into all official languages of the Union becomes available, a request for unitary effect as referred to in Article 9 of Regulation (EU) No 1257/2012 should be accompanied by a full translation of the specification of the patent into English where the language of the proceedings before the EPO is French or German, or into any official language of the Member States that is an official language of the Union where the language of the proceedings before the EPO is English. Those arrangements would ensure that during a transitional period all European patents with unitary effect are made available in English which is the language customarily used in the field of international technological research and publications. Furthermore, such arrangements would ensure that with respect to European patents with unitary effect, translations would be published in other official languages of the participating Member States. Such translations should not be carried out by automated means and their high quality should contribute to the training of translation engines by the EPO. They would also enhance the dissemination of patent information.

(13) The transitional period should terminate as soon as high quality machine translations into all official languages of the Union are available, subject to a regular and objective evaluation of the quality by an independent expert committee established by the participating Member States in the framework of the European Patent Organisation and composed of the representatives of the EPO and the users of the European patent system. Given the state of technological development, the maximum period for the development of high quality machine translations cannot be considered to exceed 12 years. Consequently, the transitional period should lapse 12 years from the date of application of this Regulation, unless it has been decided to terminate that period earlier.

(14) Since the substantive provisions applicable to a European patent with unitary effect are governed by Regulation (EU) No 1257/2012 and are completed by the translation arrangements provided for in this Regulation, this Regulation should apply from the same date as Regulation (EU) No 1257/2012.

(15) This Regulation is without prejudice to the rules governing of the Institutions of the Union established in accordance with Article 342 of the TFEU and to Council Regulation No 1 of 15 April 1958 determining the languages to be used by the European Economic Community (3). This Regulation is based on the linguistic regime of the EPO and should not be considered as creating a specific linguistic regime for the Union, or as creating a precedent for a limited language regime in any future legal instrument of the Union.

(16) Since the objective of this Regulation, namely the creation of a uniform and simple translation regime for European patents with unitary effect, cannot be sufficiently achieved by the Member States and can therefore, by reasons of the scale and effects of this Regulation, be better achieved at Union level, the Union may adopt measures, where appropriate by means of enhanced cooperation, in accordance with the principle of subsidiarity as set out in Article 5 of the Treaty on European Union. In accordance with the principle of proportionality, as set out in that Article, this Regulation does not go beyond what is necessary in order to achieve that objective,

HAS ADOPTED THIS REGULATION:

Article 1
Subject matter

This Regulation implements enhanced cooperation in the area of the creation of unitary patent protection authorised by Decision No 2011/167/EU with regard to the applicable translation arrangements.

Article 2
Definitions

For the purposes of this Regulation, the following definitions shall apply:

(a) 'European patent with unitary effect' means a European patent which benefits from unitary effect in the participating Member States by virtue of Regulation (EU) No 1257/2012;

(b) 'Language of the proceedings' means the language used in the proceedings before the EPO as defined in Article 14(3) of the Convention on the Grant of European Patents of 5 October 1973, as revised on 17 December 1991 and on 29 November 2000 (hereinafter 'EPC').

Article 3
Translation arrangements for the European patent with unitary effect

1. Without prejudice to Articles 4 and 6 of this Regulation, where the specification of a European patent, which benefits from unitary effect has been published in accordance with Article 14(6) of the EPC, no further translations shall be required.
2. A request for unitary effect as referred to in Article 9 of Regulation (EU) No 1257/2012 shall be submitted in the language of the proceedings.

Article 4
Translation in the event of a dispute

1. In the event of a dispute relating to an alleged infringement of a European patent with unitary effect, the patent proprietor shall provide at the request and the choice of an alleged infringer, a full translation of the European patent with unitary effect into an official language of either the participating Member State in which the alleged infringement took place or the Member State in which the alleged infringer is domiciled.
2. In the event of a dispute relating to a European patent with unitary effect, the patent proprietor shall provide in the course of legal proceedings, at the request of a court competent in the participating Member States for disputes concerning European patents with unitary effect, a full translation of the patent into the language used in the proceedings of that court.
3. The cost of the translations referred to in paragraphs 1 and 2 shall be borne by the patent proprietor.
4. In the event of a dispute concerning a claim for damages, the court hearing the dispute shall assess and take into consideration, in particular where the alleged infringer is a SME, a natural person or a non-profit organisation, a university or a public research organisation, whether the alleged infringer acted without knowing or without reasonable grounds for knowing, that he was infringing the European patent with unitary effect before having been provided with the translation referred to in paragraph 1.

Article 5
Administration of a compensation scheme

1. Given the fact that European patent applications may be filed in any language under Article 14(2) of the EPC, the participating Member States shall in accordance with Article 9 of Regulation (EU) No 1257/2012, give, within the meaning of Article 143 of the EPC, the EPO the task of administering a compensation scheme for the reimbursement of all translation costs up to a ceiling, for applicants filing patent applications at the EPO in one of the official languages of the Union that is not an official language of the EPO.
2. The compensation scheme referred to in paragraph 1 shall be funded through the fees referred to in Article 11 of Regulation (EU) No 1257/2012 and shall

be available only for SMEs, natural persons, non-profit organisations, universities and public research organisations having their residence or principal place of business within a Member State.

Article 6
Transitional measures

1. During a transitional period starting on the date of application of this Regulation a request for unitary effect as referred to in Article 9 of Regulation (EU) No 1257/2012 shall be submitted together with the following:
   (a) where the language of the proceedings is French or German, a full translation of the specification of the European patent into English; or
   (b) where the language of the proceedings is English, a full translation of the specification of the European patent into any other official language of the Union.
2. In accordance with Article 9 of Regulation (EU) No 1257/2012, the participating Member States shall give, within the meaning of Article 143 of the EPC, the EPO the task of publishing the translations referred to in paragraph 1 of this Article as soon as possible after the date of the submission of a request for unitary effect as referred to in Article 9 of Regulation (EU) No 1257/2012. The text of such translations shall have no legal effect and shall be for information purposes only.
3. Six years after the date of application of this Regulation and every two years thereafter, an independent expert committee shall carry out an objective evaluation of the availability of high quality machine translations of patent applications and specifications into all the official languages of the Union as developed by the EPO. This expert committee shall be established by the participating Member States in the framework of the European Patent Organisation and shall be composed of representatives of the EPO and of the non-governmental organisations representing users of the European patent system invited by the Administrative Council of the European Patent Organisation as observers in accordance with Article 30(3) of the EPC.
4. On the basis of the first of the evaluations referred to in paragraph 3 of this Article and every two years thereafter on the basis of the subsequent evaluations, the Commission shall present a report to the Council and, if appropriate, make proposals for terminating the transitional period.
5. If the transitional period is not terminated on the basis of a proposal of the Commission, it shall lapse 12 years from the date of application of this Regulation.

Article 7
Entry into force

1. This Regulation shall enter into force on the twentieth day following that of its publication in the Official Journal of the European Union.

2. It shall apply from 1 January 2014 or the date of entry into force of the Agreement on a Unified Patent Court, whichever is the later.

This Regulation shall be binding in its entirety and directly applicable in the participating Member States in accordance with the Treaties.

Done at Brussels, 17 December 2012.

For the Council
The President
S. ALETRARIS

(1) OJ L76, 22.3.2011, p. 53.
(2) See page 1 of this Official Journal.
(3) OJ 17, 6.10.1958, p. 385/58.

III.

AGREEMENT ON A UNIFIED PATENT COURT

Table of Contents[1]

Agreement on a Unified Patent Court

[1] The Table of Contents has been added for the reader's convenience.

AGREEMENT on a Unified Patent Court 2013/C 175/01

THE CONTRACTING MEMBER STATES,

CONSIDERING that cooperation amongst the Member States of the European Union in the field of patents contributes significantly to the integration process in Europe, in particular to the establishment of an internal market within the European Union characterised by the free movement of goods and services and the creation of a system ensuring that competition in the internal market is not distorted;

CONSIDERING that the fragmented market for patents and the significant variations between national court systems are detrimental for innovation, in particular for small and medium-sized enterprises which have difficulties to enforce their patents and to defend themselves against unfounded claims and claims relating to patents which should be revoked;

CONSIDERING that the European Patent Convention ('EPC') which has been ratified by all Member States of the European Union provides for a single procedure for granting European patents by the European Patent Office;

CONSIDERING that by virtue of Regulation (EU) No 1257/2012 (1), patent proprietors can request unitary effect of their European patents so as to obtain unitary patent protection in the Member States of the European Union participating in the enhanced cooperation;

WISHING to improve the enforcement of patents and the defence against unfounded claims and patents which should be revoked and to enhance legal certainty by setting up a Unified Patent Court for litigation relating to the infringement and validity of patents;

CONSIDERING that the Unified Patent Court should be devised to ensure expeditious and high quality decisions, striking a fair balance between the interests of right holders and other parties and taking into account the need for proportionality and flexibility;

CONSIDERING that the Unified Patent Court should be a court common to the Contracting Member States and thus part of their judicial system, with exclusive competence in respect of European patents with unitary effect and European patents granted under the provisions of the EPC;

CONSIDERING that the Court of Justice of the European Union is to ensure the uniformity of the Union legal order and the primacy of European Union law;

RECALLING the obligations of the Contracting Member States under the Treaty on European Union (TEU) and the Treaty on the Functioning of the European Union (TFEU), including the obligation of sincere cooperation as set out in Article 4(3) TEU and the obligation to ensure through the Unified Patent Court the full application of, and respect for, Union law in their respective territories and the judicial protection of an individual's rights under that law;

CONSIDERING that, as any national court, the Unified Patent Court must respect and apply Union law and, in collaboration with the Court of Justice of the European Union as guardian of Union law, ensure its correct application and uniform interpretation; the Unified Patent Court must in particular cooperate with the Court of Justice of the European Union in properly interpreting Union law by relying on the latter's case law and by requesting preliminary rulings in accordance with Article 267 TFEU;

CONSIDERING that the Contracting Member States should, in line with the case law of the Court of Justice of the European Union on non-contractual liability, be liable for damages caused by infringements of Union law by the Unified Patent Court, including the failure to request preliminary rulings from the Court of Justice of the European Union;

CONSIDERING that infringements of Union law by the Unified Patent Court, including the failure to request preliminary rulings from the Court of Justice of the European Union, are directly attributable to the Contracting Member States and infringement proceedings can therefore be brought under Article 258, 259 and 260 TFEU against any Contracting Member State to ensure the respect of the primacy and proper application of Union law;

RECALLING the primacy of Union law, which includes the TEU, the TFEU, the Charter of Fundamental Rights of the European Union, the general principles of Union law as developed by the Court of Justice of the European Union, and in particular the right to an effective remedy before a tribunal and a fair and public hearing within a reasonable time by an independent and impartial tribunal, the case law of the Court of Justice of the European Union and secondary Union law;

CONSIDERING that this Agreement should be open to accession by any Member State of the European Union; Member States which have decided not to participate in the enhanced cooperation in the area of the creation of unitary patent protection may participate in this Agreement in respect of European patents granted for their respective territory;

CONSIDERING that this Agreement should enter into force on 1 January 2014 or on the first day of the fourth month after the 13th deposit, provided that the Contracting Member States that will have deposited their instruments of ratification or accession include the three States in which the highest number of European patents was in force in the year preceding the year in which the signature of the Agreement takes place, or on the first day of the fourth month after the date of entry into force of the amendments to Regulation (EU) No 1215/2012 (2) concerning its relationship with this Agreement, whichever is the latest,

HAVE AGREED AS FOLLOWS:

PART I
GENERAL AND INSTITUTIONAL PROVISIONS

CHAPTER I

GENERAL PROVISIONS

Article 1
Unified Patent Court

A Unified Patent Court for the settlement of disputes relating to European patents and European patents with unitary effect is hereby established.

The Unified Patent Court shall be a court common to the Contracting Member States and thus subject to the same obligations under Union law as any national court of the Contracting Member States.

Article 2
Definitions

For the purposes of this Agreement:

(a) 'Court' means the Unified Patent Court created by this Agreement.
(b) 'Member State' means a Member State of the European Union.
(c) 'Contracting Member State' means a Member State party to this Agreement.
(d) 'EPC' means the Convention on the Grant of European Patents of 5 October 1973, including any subsequent amendments.
(e) 'European patent' means a patent granted under the provisions of the EPC, which does not benefit from unitary effect by virtue of Regulation (EU) No 1257/2012.
(f) 'European patent with unitary effect' means a patent granted under the provisions of the EPC which benefits from unitary effect by virtue of Regulation (EU) No 1257/2012.
(g) 'Patent' means a European patent and/or a European patent with unitary effect.
(h) 'Supplementary protection certificate' means a supplementary protection certificate granted under Regulation (EC) No 469/2009 (3) or under Regulation (EC) No 1610/96 (4).
(i) 'Statute' means the Statute of the Court as set out in Annex I, which shall be an integral part of this Agreement.
(j) 'Rules of Procedure' means the Rules of Procedure of the Court, as established in accordance with Article 41.

Article 3
Scope of application

This Agreement shall apply to any:

(a) European patent with unitary effect;
(b) supplementary protection certificate issued for a product protected by a patent;
(c) European patent which has not yet lapsed at the date of entry into force of this Agreement or was granted after that date, without prejudice to Article 83; and
(d) European patent application which is pending at the date of entry into force of this Agreement or which is filed after that date, without prejudice to Article 83.

Article 4
Legal status

1. The Court shall have legal personality in each Contracting Member State and shall enjoy the most extensive legal capacity accorded to legal persons under the national law of that State.
2. The Court shall be represented by the President of the Court of Appeal who shall be elected in accordance with the Statute.

Article 5
Liability

1. The contractual liability of the Court shall be governed by the law applicable to the contract in question in accordance with Regulation (EC) No 593/2008 (5) (Rome I), where applicable, or failing that in accordance with the law of the Member State of the court seized.
2. The non-contractual liability of the Court in respect of any damage caused by it or its staff in the performance of their duties, to the extent that it is not a civil and commercial matter within the meaning of Regulation (EC) No 864/2007 (6) (Rome II), shall be governed by the law of the Contracting Member State in which the damage occurred. This provision is without prejudice to the application of Article 22.
3. The court with jurisdiction to settle disputes under paragraph 2 shall be a court of the Contracting Member State in which the damage occurred.

CHAPTER II

INSTITUTIONAL PROVISIONS

Article 6
The Court

1. The Court shall comprise a Court of First Instance, a Court of Appeal and a Registry.
2. The Court shall perform the functions assigned to it by this Agreement.

Article 7
The Court of First Instance

1. The Court of First Instance shall comprise a central division as well as local and regional divisions.
2. The central division shall have its seat in Paris, with sections in London and Munich. The cases before the central division shall be distributed in accordance with Annex II, which shall form an integral part of this Agreement.
3. A local division shall be set up in a Contracting Member State upon its request in accordance with the Statute. A Contracting Member State hosting a local division shall designate its seat.
4. An additional local division shall be set up in a Contracting Member State upon its request for every one hundred patent cases per calendar year that have been commenced in that Contracting Member State during three successive years prior to or subsequent to the date of entry into force of this Agreement. The number of local divisions in one Contracting Member State shall not exceed four.
5. A regional division shall be set up for two or more Contracting Member States, upon their request in accordance with the Statute. Such Contracting Member States shall designate the seat of the division concerned. The regional division may hear cases in multiple locations.

Article 8
Composition of the panels of the Court of First Instance

1. Any panel of the Court of First Instance shall have a multinational composition. Without prejudice to paragraph 5 of this Article and to Article 33(3)(a), it shall sit in a composition of three judges.
2. Any panel of a local division in a Contracting Member State where, during a period of three successive years prior or subsequent to the entry into force of this Agreement, less than fifty patent cases per calendar year on average have been commenced shall sit in a composition of one legally qualified judge who is a national of the Contracting Member State hosting the local division concerned and two legally qualified judges who are not nationals of

the Contracting Member State concerned and are allocated from the Pool of Judges in accordance with Article 18(3) on a case by case basis.

3. Notwithstanding paragraph 2, any panel of a local division in a Contracting Member State where, during a period of three successive years prior or subsequent to the entry into force of this Agreement, fifty or more patent cases per calendar year on average have been commenced, shall sit in a composition of two legally qualified judges who are nationals of the Contracting Member State hosting the local division concerned and one legally qualified judge who is not a national of the Contracting Member State concerned and is allocated from the Pool of Judges in accordance with Article 18(3). Such third judge shall serve at the local division on a long term basis, where this is necessary for the efficient functioning of divisions with a high work load.
4. Any panel of a regional division shall sit in a composition of two legally qualified judges chosen from a regional list of judges, who shall be nationals of the Contracting Member States concerned, and one legally qualified judge who shall not be a national of the Contracting Member States concerned and who shall be allocated from the Pool of Judges in accordance with Article 18(3).
5. Upon request by one of the parties, any panel of a local or regional division shall request the President of the Court of First Instance to allocate from the Pool of Judges in accordance with Article 18(3) an additional technically qualified judge with qualifications and experience in the field of technology concerned. Moreover, any panel of a local or regional division may, after having heard the parties, submit such request on its own initiative, where it deems this appropriate.

   In cases where such a technically qualified judge is allocated, no further technically qualified judge may be allocated under Article 33(3)(a).
6. Any panel of the central division shall sit in a composition of two legally qualified judges who are nationals of different Contracting Member States and one technically qualified judge allocated from the Pool of Judges in accordance with Article 18(3) with qualifications and experience in the field of technology concerned. However, any panel of the central division dealing with actions under Article 32(1)(i) shall sit in a composition of three legally qualified judges who are nationals of different Contracting Member States.
7. Notwithstanding paragraphs 1 to 6 and in accordance with the Rules of Procedure, parties may agree to have their case heard by a single legally qualified judge.
8. Any panel of the Court of First Instance shall be chaired by a legally qualified judge.

Article 9
The Court of Appeal

1. Any panel of the Court of Appeal shall sit in a multinational composition of five judges. It shall sit in a composition of three legally qualified judges who are

nationals of different Contracting Member States and two technically qualified judges with qualifications and experience in the field of technology concerned. Those technically qualified judges shall be assigned to the panel by the President of the Court of Appeal from the pool of judges in accordance with Article 18.

2. Notwithstanding paragraph 1, a panel dealing with actions under Article 32(1)(i) shall sit in a composition of three legally qualified judges who are nationals of different Contracting Member States.
3. Any panel of the Court of Appeal shall be chaired by a legally qualified judge.
4. The panels of the Court of Appeal shall be set up in accordance with the Statute.
5. The Court of Appeal shall have its seat in Luxembourg.

Article 10
The Registry

1. A Registry shall be set up at the seat of the Court of Appeal. It shall be managed by the Registrar and perform the functions assigned to it in accordance with the Statute. Subject to conditions set out in this Agreement and the Rules of Procedure, the register kept by the Registry shall be public.
2. Sub-registries shall be set up at all divisions of the Court of First Instance.
3. The Registry shall keep records of all cases before the Court. Upon filing, the sub-registry concerned shall notify every case to the Registry.
4. The Court shall appoint the Registrar in accordance with Article 22 of the Statute and lay down the rules governing the Registrar's service.

Article 11
Committees

An Administrative Committee, a Budget Committee and an Advisory Committee shall be set up in order to ensure the effective implementation and operation of this Agreement. They shall in particular exercise the duties foreseen by this Agreement and the Statute.

Article 12
The Administrative Committee

1. The Administrative Committee shall be composed of one representative of each Contracting Member State. The European Commission shall be represented at the meetings of the Administrative Committee as observer.
2. Each Contracting Member State shall have one vote.
3. The Administrative Committee shall adopt its decisions by a majority of three quarters of the Contracting Member States represented and voting, except where this Agreement or the Statute provides otherwise.
4. The Administrative Committee shall adopt its rules of procedure.
5. The Administrative Committee shall elect a chairperson from among its members for a term of three years. That term shall be renewable.

Article 13
The Budget Committee

1. The Budget Committee shall be composed of one representative of each Contracting Member State.
2. Each Contracting Member State shall have one vote.
3. The Budget Committee shall take its decisions by a simple majority of the representatives of the Contracting Member States. However, a majority of three-quarters of the representatives of Contracting Member States shall be required for the adoption of the budget.
4. The Budget Committee shall adopt its rules of procedure.
5. The Budget Committee shall elect a chairperson from among its members for a term of three years. That term shall be renewable.

Article 14
The Advisory Committee

1. The Advisory Committee shall:
   (a) assist the Administrative Committee in the preparation of the appointment of judges of the Court;
   (b) make proposals to the Presidium referred to in Article 15 of the Statute on the guidelines for the training framework for judges referred to in Article 19; and
   (c) deliver opinions to the Administrative Committee concerning the requirements for qualifications referred to in Article 48(2).
2. The Advisory Committee shall comprise patent judges and practitioners in patent law and patent litigation with the highest recognised competence. They shall be appointed, in accordance with the procedure laid down in the Statute, for a term of six years. That term shall be renewable.
3. The composition of the Advisory Committee shall ensure a broad range of relevant expertise and the representation of each of the Contracting Member States. The members of the Advisory Committee shall be completely independent in the performance of their duties and shall not be bound by any instructions.
4. The Advisory Committee shall adopt its rules of procedure.
5. The Advisory Committee shall elect a chairperson from among its members for a term of three years. That term shall be renewable.

CHAPTER III

JUDGES OF THE COURT

Article 15
Eligibility criteria for the appointment of judges

1. The Court shall comprise both legally qualified judges and technically qualified judges. Judges shall ensure the highest standards of competence and shall have proven experience in the field of patent litigation.
2. Legally qualified judges shall possess the qualifications required for appointment to judicial offices in a Contracting Member State.
3. Technically qualified judges shall have a university degree and proven expertise in a field of technology. They shall also have proven knowledge of civil law and procedure relevant in patent litigation.

Article 16
Appointment procedure

1. The Advisory Committee shall establish a list of the most suitable candidates to be appointed as judges of the Court, in accordance with the Statute.
2. On the basis of that list, the Administrative Committee shall appoint the judges of the Court acting by common accord.
3. The implementing provisions for the appointment of judges are set out in the Statute.

Article 17
Judicial independence and impartiality

1. The Court, its judges and the Registrar shall enjoy judicial independence. In the performance of their duties, the judges shall not be bound by any instructions.
2. Legally qualified judges, as well as technically qualified judges who are full-time judges of the Court, may not engage in any other occupation, whether gainful or not, unless an exception is granted by the Administrative Committee.
3. Notwithstanding paragraph 2, the exercise of the office of judges shall not exclude the exercise of other judicial functions at national level.
4. The exercise of the office of technically qualified judges who are part-time judges of the Court shall not exclude the exercise of other functions provided there is no conflict of interest.
5. In case of a conflict of interest, the judge concerned shall not take part in proceedings. Rules governing conflicts of interest are set out in the Statute.

Article 18
Pool of Judges

1. A Pool of Judges shall be established in accordance with the Statute.
2. The Pool of Judges shall be composed of all legally qualified judges and technically qualified judges from the Court of First Instance who are full-time or part-time judges of the Court. The Pool of Judges shall include at least one technically qualified judge per field of technology with the relevant qualifications and experience. The technically qualified judges from the Pool of Judges shall also be available to the Court of Appeal.
3. Where so provided by this Agreement or the Statute, the judges from the Pool of Judges shall be allocated to the division concerned by the President of the Court of First Instance. The allocation of judges shall be based on their legal or technical expertise, linguistic skills and relevant experience. The allocation of judges shall guarantee the same high quality of work and the same high level of legal and technical expertise in all panels of the Court of First Instance.

Article 19
Training framework

1. A training framework for judges, the details of which are set out in the Statute, shall be set up in order to improve and increase available patent litigation expertise and to ensure a broad geographic distribution of such specific knowledge and experience. The facilities for that framework shall be situated in Budapest.
2. The training framework shall in particular focus on:
   (a) internships in national patent courts or divisions of the Court of First Instance hearing a substantial number of patent litigation cases;
   (b) improvement of linguistic skills;
   (c) technical aspects of patent law;
   (d) the dissemination of knowledge and experience in civil procedure for technically qualified judges;
   (e) the preparation of candidate-judges.
3. The training framework shall provide for continuous training. Regular meetings shall be organised between all judges of the Court in order to discuss developments in patent law and to ensure the consistency of the Court's case law.

CHAPTER IV

THE PRIMACY OF UNION LAW, LIABILITY AND RESPONSIBILITY OF THE CONTRACTING MEMBER STATES

Article 20
Primacy of and respect for Union law

The Court shall apply Union law in its entirety and shall respect its primacy.

Article 21
Requests for preliminary rulings

As a court common to the Contracting Member States and as part of their judicial system, the Court shall cooperate with the Court of Justice of the European Union to ensure the correct application and uniform interpretation of Union law, as any national court, in accordance with Article 267 TFEU in particular. Decisions of the Court of Justice of the European Union shall be binding on the Court.

Article 22
Liability for damage caused by infringements of Union law

1. The Contracting Member States are jointly and severally liable for damage resulting from an infringement of Union law by the Court of Appeal, in accordance with Union law concerning non-contractual liability of Member States for damage caused by their national courts breaching Union law.
2. An action for such damages shall be brought against the Contracting Member State where the claimant has its residence or principal place of business or, in the absence of residence or principal place of business, place of business, before the competent authority of that Contracting Member State. Where the claimant does not have its residence, or principal place of business or, in the absence of residence or principal place of business, place of business in a Contracting Member State, the claimant may bring such an action against the Contracting Member State where the Court of Appeal has its seat, before the competent authority of that Contracting Member State.

The competent authority shall apply the lex fori, with the exception of its private international law, to all questions not regulated by Union law or by this Agreement. The claimant shall be entitled to obtain the entire amount of damages awarded by the competent authority from the Contracting Member State against which the action was brought.

3. The Contracting Member State that has paid damages is entitled to obtain proportional contribution, established in accordance with the method laid down in Article 37(3) and (4), from the other Contracting Member States. The detailed rules governing the Contracting Member States' contribution under this paragraph shall be determined by the Administrative Committee.

Article 23
Responsibility of the Contracting Member States

Actions of the Court are directly attributable to each Contracting Member State individually, including for the purposes of Articles 258, 259 and 260 TFEU, and to all Contracting Member States collectively.

CHAPTER V

SOURCES OF LAW AND SUBSTANTIVE LAW

Article 24
Sources of law

1. In full compliance with Article 20, when hearing a case brought before it under this Agreement, the Court shall base its decisions on:
   (a) Union law, including Regulation (EU) No 1257/2012 and Regulation (EU) No 1260/2012 (7);
   (b) this Agreement;
   (c) the EPC;
   (d) other international agreements applicable to patents and binding on all the Contracting Member States; and
   (e) national law.
2. To the extent that the Court shall base its decisions on national law, including where relevant the law of non-contracting States, the applicable law shall be determined:
   (a) by directly applicable provisions of Union law containing private international law rules, or
   (b) in the absence of directly applicable provisions of Union law or where the latter do not apply, by international instruments containing private international law rules; or
   (c) in the absence of provisions referred to in points (a) and (b), by national provisions on private international law as determined by the Court.
3. The law of non-contracting States shall apply when designated by application of the rules referred to in paragraph 2, in particular in relation to Articles 25 to 28, 54, 55, 64, 68 and 72.

Article 25
Right to prevent the direct use of the invention

A patent shall confer on its proprietor the right to prevent any third party not having the proprietor's consent from the following:

(a) making, offering, placing on the market or using a product which is the subject-matter of the patent, or importing or storing the product for those purposes;

(b) using a process which is the subject-matter of the patent or, where the third party knows, or should have known, that the use of the process is prohibited without the consent of the patent proprietor, offering the process for use within the territory of the Contracting Member States in which that patent has effect;
(c) offering, placing on the market, using, or importing or storing for those purposes a product obtained directly by a process which is the subject-matter of the patent.

Article 26
Right to prevent the indirect use of the invention

1. A patent shall confer on its proprietor the right to prevent any third party not having the proprietor's consent from supplying or offering to supply, within the territory of the Contracting Member States in which that patent has effect, any person other than a party entitled to exploit the patented invention, with means, relating to an essential element of that invention, for putting it into effect therein, when the third party knows, or should have known, that those means are suitable and intended for putting that invention into effect.
2. Paragraph 1 shall not apply when the means are staple commercial products, except where the third party induces the person supplied to perform any of the acts prohibited by Article 25.
3. Persons performing the acts referred to in Article 27(a) to (e) shall not be considered to be parties entitled to exploit the invention within the meaning of paragraph 1.

Article 27
Limitations of the effects of a patent

The rights conferred by a patent shall not extend to any of the following:

(a) acts done privately and for non-commercial purposes;
(b) acts done for experimental purposes relating to the subject-matter of the patented invention;
(c) the use of biological material for the purpose of breeding, or discovering and developing other plant varieties;
(d) the acts allowed pursuant to Article 13(6) of Directive 2001/82/EC (8) or Article 10(6) of Directive 2001/83/EC (9) in respect of any patent covering the product within the meaning of either of those Directives;
(e) the extemporaneous preparation by a pharmacy, for individual cases, of a medicine in accordance with a medical prescription or acts concerning the medicine so prepared;
(f) the use of the patented invention on board vessels of countries of the International Union for the Protection of Industrial Property (Paris Union) or members of the World Trade Organisation, other than those Contracting Member States in which that patent has effect, in the body of such vessel,

in the machinery, tackle, gear and other accessories, when such vessels temporarily or accidentally enter the waters of a Contracting Member State in which that patent has effect, provided that the invention is used there exclusively for the needs of the vessel;

(g) the use of the patented invention in the construction or operation of aircraft or land vehicles or other means of transport of countries of the International Union for the Protection of Industrial Property (Paris Union) or members of the World Trade Organisation, other than those Contracting Member States in which that patent has effect, or of accessories to such aircraft or land vehicles, when these temporarily or accidentally enter the territory of a Contracting Member State in which that patent has effect;

(h) the acts specified in Article 27 of the Convention on International Civil Aviation of 7 December 1944 (10), where these acts concern the aircraft of a country party to that Convention other than a Contracting Member State in which that patent has effect;

(i) the use by a farmer of the product of his harvest for propagation or multiplication by him on his own holding, provided that the plant propagating material was sold or otherwise commercialised to the farmer by or with the consent of the patent proprietor for agricultural use. The extent and the conditions for this use correspond to those under Article 14 of Regulation (EC) No 2100/94 (11);

(j) the use by a farmer of protected livestock for an agricultural purpose, provided that the breeding stock or other animal reproductive material were sold or otherwise commercialised to the farmer by or with the consent of the patent proprietor. Such use includes making the animal or other animal reproductive material available for the purposes of pursuing the farmer's agricultural activity, but not the sale thereof within the framework of, or for the purpose of, a commercial reproductive activity;

(k) the acts and the use of the obtained information as allowed under Articles 5 and 6 of Directive 2009/24/EC (12), in particular, by its provisions on decompilation and interoperability; and

(l) the acts allowed pursuant to Article 10 of Directive 98/44/EC (13).

Article 28
Right based on prior use of the invention

Any person, who, if a national patent had been granted in respect of an invention, would have had, in a Contracting Member State, a right based on prior use of that invention or a right of personal possession of that invention, shall enjoy, in that Contracting Member State, the same rights in respect of a patent for the same invention.

Article 29
Exhaustion of the rights conferred by a European patent

The rights conferred by a European patent shall not extend to acts concerning a product covered by that patent after that product has been placed on the market in the European Union by, or with the consent of, the patent proprietor, unless there are legitimate grounds for the patent proprietor to oppose further commercialisation of the product.

Article 30
Effects of supplementary protection certificates

A supplementary protection certificate shall confer the same rights as conferred by the patent and shall be subject to the same limitations and the same obligations.

CHAPTER VI

INTERNATIONAL JURISDICTION AND COMPETENCE

Article 31
International jurisdiction

The international jurisdiction of the Court shall be established in accordance with Regulation (EU) No 1215/2012 or, where applicable, on the basis of the Convention on jurisdiction and the recognition and enforcement of judgments in civil and commercial matters (Lugano Convention) (14).

Article 32
Competence of the Court

1. The Court shall have exclusive competence in respect of:
    (a) actions for actual or threatened infringements of patents and supplementary protection certificates and related defences, including counterclaims concerning licences;
    (b) actions for declarations of non-infringement of patents and supplementary protection certificates;
    (c) actions for provisional and protective measures and injunctions;
    (d) actions for revocation of patents and for declaration of invalidity of supplementary protection certificates;
    (e) counterclaims for revocation of patents and for declaration of invalidity of supplementary protection certificates;
    (f) actions for damages or compensation derived from the provisional protection conferred by a published European patent application;
    (g) actions relating to the use of the invention prior to the granting of the patent or to the right based on prior use of the invention;

(h) actions for compensation for licences on the basis of Article 8 of Regulation (EU) No 1257/2012; and
(i) actions concerning decisions of the European Patent Office in carrying out the tasks referred to in Article 9 of Regulation (EU) No 1257/2012.

2. The national courts of the Contracting Member States shall remain competent for actions relating to patents and supplementary protection certificates which do not come within the exclusive competence of the Court.

Article 33
Competence of the divisions of the Court of First Instance

1. Without prejudice to paragraph 7 of this Article, actions referred to in Article 32(1)(a), (c), (f) and (g) shall be brought before:
   (a) the local division hosted by the Contracting Member State where the actual or threatened infringement has occurred or may occur, or the regional division in which that Contracting Member State participates; or
   (b) the local division hosted by the Contracting Member State where the defendant or, in the case of multiple defendants, one of the defendants has its residence, or principal place of business, or in the absence of residence or principal place of business, its place of business, or the regional division in which that Contracting Member State participates. An action may be brought against multiple defendants only where the defendants have a commercial relationship and where the action relates to the same alleged infringement.

Actions referred to in Article 32(1)(h) shall be brought before the local or regional division in accordance with point (b) of the first subparagraph.

Actions against defendants having their residence, or principal place of business or, in the absence of residence or principal place of business, their place of business, outside the territory of the Contracting Member States shall be brought before the local or regional division in accordance with point (a) of the first subparagraph or before the central division.

If the Contracting Member State concerned does not host a local division and does not participate in a regional division, actions shall be brought before the central division.

2. If an action referred to in Article 32(1)(a), (c), (f), (g) or (h) is pending before a division of the Court of First Instance, any action referred to in Article 32(1)(a), (c), (f), (g) or (h) between the same parties on the same patent may not be brought before any other division.

If an action referred to in Article 32(1)(a) is pending before a regional division and the infringement has occurred in the territories of three or more regional divisions, the regional division concerned shall, at the request of the defendant, refer the case to the central division.

In case an action between the same parties on the same patent is brought before several different divisions, the division first seized shall be competent for the whole case and any division seized later shall declare the action inadmissible in accordance with the Rules of Procedure.

3. A counterclaim for revocation as referred to in Article 32(1)(e) may be brought in the case of an action for infringement as referred to in Article 32(1)(a). The local or regional division concerned shall, after having heard the parties, have the discretion either to:
   (a) proceed with both the action for infringement and with the counterclaim for revocation and request the President of the Court of First Instance to allocate from the Pool of Judges in accordance with Article 18(3) a technically qualified judge with qualifications and experience in the field of technology concerned.
   (b) refer the counterclaim for revocation for decision to the central division and suspend or proceed with the action for infringement; or
   (c) with the agreement of the parties, refer the case for decision to the central division.
4. Actions referred to in Article 32(1)(b) and (d) shall be brought before the central division. If, however, an action for infringement as referred to in Article 32(1)(a) between the same parties relating to the same patent has been brought before a local or a regional division, these actions may only be brought before the same local or regional division.
5. If an action for revocation as referred to in Article 32(1)(d) is pending before the central division, an action for infringement as referred to in Article 32(1)(a) between the same parties relating to the same patent may be brought before any division in accordance with paragraph 1 of this Article or before the central division. The local or regional division concerned shall have the discretion to proceed in accordance with paragraph 3 of this Article.
6. An action for declaration of non-infringement as referred to in Article 32(1)(b) pending before the central division shall be stayed once an infringement action as referred to in Article 32(1)(a) between the same parties or between the holder of an exclusive licence and the party requesting a declaration of non-infringement relating to the same patent is brought before a local or regional division within three months of the date on which the action was initiated before the central division.
7. Parties may agree to bring actions referred to in Article 32(1)(a) to (h) before the division of their choice, including the central division.
8. Actions referred to in Article 32(1)(d) and (e) can be brought without the applicant having to file notice of opposition with the European Patent Office.
9. Actions referred to in Article 32(1)(i) shall be brought before the central division.

10. A party shall inform the Court of any pending revocation, limitation or opposition proceedings before the European Patent Office, and of any request for accelerated processing before the European Patent Office. The Court may stay its proceedings when a rapid decision may be expected from the European Patent Office.

Article 34
Territorial scope of decisions

Decisions of the Court shall cover, in the case of a European patent, the territory of those Contracting Member States for which the European patent has effect.

CHAPTER VII

PATENT MEDIATION AND ARBITRATION

Article 35
Patent mediation and arbitration centre

1. A patent mediation and arbitration centre ('the Centre') is hereby established. It shall have its seats in Ljubljana and Lisbon.
2. The Centre shall provide facilities for mediation and arbitration of patent disputes falling within the scope of this Agreement. Article 82 shall apply mutatis mutandis to any settlement reached through the use of the facilities of the Centre, including through mediation. However, a patent may not be revoked or limited in mediation or arbitration proceedings.
3. The Centre shall establish Mediation and Arbitration Rules.
4. The Centre shall draw up a list of mediators and arbitrators to assist the parties in the settlement of their dispute.

PART II
FINANCIAL PROVISIONS

Article 36
Budget of the Court

1. The budget of the Court shall be financed by the Court's own financial revenues and, at least in the transitional period referred to in Article 83 as necessary, by contributions from the Contracting Member States. The budget shall be balanced.
2. The Court's own financial revenues shall comprise court fees and other revenues.
3. Court fees shall be fixed by the Administrative Committee. They shall consist of a fixed fee, combined with a value-based fee above a pre-defined ceiling. The Court fees shall be fixed at such a level as to ensure a right balance

between the principle of fair access to justice, in particular for small and medium-sized enterprises, micro-entities, natural persons, non-profit organisations, universities and public research organisations and an adequate contribution of the parties for the costs incurred by the Court, recognising the economic benefits to the parties involved, and the objective of a self-financing Court with balanced finances. The level of the Court fees shall be reviewed periodically by the Administrative Committee. Targeted support measures for small and medium-sized enterprises and micro entities may be considered.

4. If the Court is unable to balance its budget out of its own resources, the Contracting Member States shall remit to it special financial contributions.

Article 37
Financing of the Court

1. The operating costs of the Court shall be covered by the budget of the Court, in accordance with the Statute.

Contracting Member States setting up a local division shall provide the facilities necessary for that purpose. Contracting Member States sharing a regional division shall provide jointly the facilities necessary for that purpose. Contracting Member States hosting the central division, its sections or the Court of Appeal shall provide the facilities necessary for that purpose. During an initial transitional period of seven years starting from the date of the entry into force of this Agreement, the Contracting Member States concerned shall also provide administrative support staff, without prejudice to the Statute of that staff.

2. On the date of entry into force of this Agreement, the Contracting Member States shall provide the initial financial contributions necessary for the setting up of the Court.
3. During the initial transitional period of seven years, starting from the date of the entry into force of this Agreement, the contribution by each Contracting Member State having ratified or acceded to the Agreement before the entry into force thereof shall be calculated on the basis of the number of European patents having effect in the territory of that State on the date of entry into force of this Agreement and the number of European patents with respect to which actions for infringement or for revocation have been brought before the national courts of that State in the three years preceding entry into force of this Agreement.

During the same initial transitional period of seven years, for Member States which ratify, or accede to, this Agreement after the entry into force thereof, the contributions shall be calculated on the basis of the number of European patents having effect in the territory of the ratifying or acceding Member State on the date of the ratification or accession and the number of European patents with respect to which actions for infringement or for revocation have been brought before the national courts of the ratifying or acceding Member State in the three years preceding the ratification or accession.

4. After the end of the initial transitional period of seven years, by which the Court is expected to have become self-financing, should contributions by the Contracting Member States become necessary, they shall be determined in accordance with the scale for the distribution of annual renewal fees for European patents with unitary effect applicable at the time the contribution becomes necessary.

Article 38
Financing of the training framework for judges

The training framework for judges shall be financed by the budget of the Court.

Article 39
Financing of the Centre

The operating costs of the Centre shall be financed by the budget of the Court.

PART III
ORGANISATION AND PROCEDURAL PROVISIONS

CHAPTER I

GENERAL PROVISIONS

Article 40
Statute

1. The Statute shall lay down the details of the organisation and functioning of the Court.
2. The Statute is annexed to this Agreement. The Statute may be amended by decision of the Administrative Committee, on the basis of a proposal of the Court or a proposal of a Contracting Member State after consultation with the Court. However, such amendments shall not contradict or alter this Agreement.
3. The Statute shall guarantee that the functioning of the Court is organised in the most efficient and cost-effective manner and shall ensure equitable access to justice.

Article 41
Rules of Procedure

1. The Rules of Procedure shall lay down the details of the proceedings before the Court. They shall comply with this Agreement and the Statute.
2. The Rules of Procedure shall be adopted by the Administrative Committee on the basis of broad consultations with stakeholders. The prior opinion of the European Commission on the compatibility of the Rules of Procedure with Union law shall be requested.

The Rules of Procedure may be amended by a decision of the Administrative Committee, on the basis of a proposal from the Court and after consultation with the European Commission. However, such amendments shall not contradict or alter this Agreement or the Statute.

3. The Rules of Procedure shall guarantee that the decisions of the Court are of the highest quality and that proceedings are organised in the most efficient and cost effective manner. They shall ensure a fair balance between the legitimate interests of all parties. They shall provide for the required level of discretion of judges without impairing the predictability of proceedings for the parties.

Article 42
Proportionality and fairness

1. The Court shall deal with litigation in ways which are proportionate to the importance and complexity thereof.
2. The Court shall ensure that the rules, procedures and remedies provided for in this Agreement and in the Statute are used in a fair and equitable manner and do not distort competition.

Article 43
Case management

The Court shall actively manage the cases before it in accordance with the Rules of Procedure without impairing the freedom of the parties to determine the subject-matter of, and the supporting evidence for, their case.

Article 44
Electronic procedures

The Court shall make best use of electronic procedures, such as the electronic filing of submissions of the parties and stating of evidence in electronic form, as well as video conferencing, in accordance with the Rules of Procedure.

Article 45
Public proceedings

The proceedings shall be open to the public unless the Court decides to make them confidential, to the extent necessary, in the interest of one of the parties or other affected persons, or in the general interest of justice or public order.

Article 46
Legal capacity

Any natural or legal person, or any body equivalent to a legal person entitled to initiate proceedings in accordance with its national law, shall have the capacity to be a party to the proceedings before the Court.

Article 47
Parties

1. The patent proprietor shall be entitled to bring actions before the Court.
2. Unless the licensing agreement provides otherwise, the holder of an exclusive licence in respect of a patent shall be entitled to bring actions before the Court under the same circumstances as the patent proprietor, provided that the patent proprietor is given prior notice.
3. The holder of a non-exclusive licence shall not be entitled to bring actions before the Court, unless the patent proprietor is given prior notice and in so far as expressly permitted by the licence agreement.
4. In actions brought by a licence holder, the patent proprietor shall be entitled to join the action before the Court.
5. The validity of a patent cannot be contested in an action for infringement brought by the holder of a licence where the patent proprietor does not take part in the proceedings. The party in an action for infringement wanting to contest the validity of a patent shall have to bring actions against the patent proprietor.
6. Any other natural or legal person, or any body entitled to bring actions in accordance with its national law, who is concerned by a patent, may bring actions in accordance with the Rules of Procedure.
7. Any natural or legal person, or any body entitled to bring actions in accordance with its national law and who is affected by a decision of the European Patent Office in carrying out the tasks referred to in Article 9 of Regulation (EU) No 1257/2012 is entitled to bring actions under Article 32(1)(i).

Article 48
Representation

1. Parties shall be represented by lawyers authorised to practise before a court of a Contracting Member State.
2. Parties may alternatively be represented by European Patent Attorneys who are entitled to act as professional representatives before the European Patent Office pursuant to Article 134 of the EPC and who have appropriate qualifications such as a European Patent Litigation Certificate.
3. The requirements for qualifications pursuant to paragraph 2 shall be established by the Administrative Committee. A list of European Patent Attorneys entitled to represent parties before the Court shall be kept by the Registrar.
4. Representatives of the parties may be assisted by patent attorneys, who shall be allowed to speak at hearings of the Court in accordance with the Rules of Procedure.
5. Representatives of the parties shall enjoy the rights and immunities necessary for the independent exercise of their duties, including the privilege from disclosure in proceedings before the Court in respect of communications

between a representative and the party or any other person, under the conditions laid down in the Rules of Procedure, unless such privilege is expressly waived by the party concerned.

6. Representatives of the parties shall be obliged not to misrepresent cases or facts before the Court either knowingly or with good reasons to know.
7. Representation in accordance with paragraphs 1 and 2 of this Article shall not be required in proceedings under Article 32(1)(i).

CHAPTER II

LANGUAGE OF PROCEEDINGS

Article 49
Language of proceedings at the Court of First Instance

1. The language of proceedings before any local or regional division shall be an official European Union language which is the official language or one of the official languages of the Contracting Member State hosting the relevant division, or the official language(s) designated by Contracting Member States sharing a regional division.
2. Notwithstanding paragraph 1, Contracting Member States may designate one or more of the official languages of the European Patent Office as the language of proceedings of their local or regional division.
3. The parties may agree on the use of the language in which the patent was granted as the language of proceedings, subject to approval by the competent panel. If the panel does not approve their choice, the parties may request that the case be referred to the central division.
4. With the agreement of the parties the competent panel may, on grounds of convenience and fairness, decide on the use of the language in which the patent was granted as the language of proceedings.
5. At the request of one of the parties and after having heard the other parties and the competent panel, the President of the Court of First Instance may, on grounds of fairness and taking into account all relevant circumstances, including the position of parties, in particular the position of the defendant, decide on the use of the language in which the patent was granted as language of proceedings. In this case the President of the Court of First Instance shall assess the need for specific translation and interpretation arrangements.
6. The language of proceedings at the central division shall be the language in which the patent concerned was granted.

Article 50
Language of proceedings at the Court of Appeal

1. The language of proceedings before the Court of Appeal shall be the language of proceedings before the Court of First Instance.
2. Notwithstanding paragraph 1 the parties may agree on the use of the language in which the patent was granted as the language of proceedings.
3. In exceptional cases and to the extent deemed appropriate, the Court of Appeal may decide on another official language of a Contracting Member State as the language of proceedings for the whole or part of the proceedings, subject to agreement by the parties.

Article 51
Other language arrangements

1. Any panel of the Court of First Instance and the Court of Appeal may, to the extent deemed appropriate, dispense with translation requirements.
2. At the request of one of the parties, and to the extent deemed appropriate, any division of the Court of First Instance and the Court of Appeal shall provide interpretation facilities to assist the parties concerned at oral proceedings.
3. Notwithstanding Article 49(6), in cases where an action for infringement is brought before the central division, a defendant having its residence, principal place of business or place of business in a Member State shall have the right to obtain, upon request, translations of relevant documents in the language of the Member State of residence, principal place of business or, in the absence of residence or principal place of business, place of business, in the following circumstances:
   (a) jurisdiction is entrusted to the central division in accordance with Article 33(1) third or fourth subparagraph, and
   (b) the language of proceedings at the central division is a language which is not an official language of the Member State where the defendant has its residence, principal place of business or, in the absence of residence or principal place of business, place of business, and
   (c) the defendant does not have proper knowledge of the language of the proceedings.

CHAPTER III

PROCEEDINGS BEFORE THE COURT

Article 52
Written, interim and oral procedures

1. The proceedings before the Court shall consist of a written, an interim and an oral procedure, in accordance with the Rules of Procedure. All procedures shall be organized in a flexible and balanced manner.

2. In the interim procedure, after the written procedure and if appropriate, the judge acting as Rapporteur, subject to a mandate of the full panel, shall be responsible for convening an interim hearing. That judge shall in particular explore with the parties the possibility for a settlement, including through mediation, and/or arbitration, by using the facilities of the Centre referred to in Article 35.
3. The oral procedure shall give parties the opportunity to explain properly their arguments. The Court may, with the agreement of the parties, dispense with the oral hearing.

Article 53
Means of evidence

1. In proceedings before the Court, the means of giving or obtaining evidence shall include in particular the following:
   (a) hearing the parties;
   (b) requests for information;
   (c) production of documents;
   (d) hearing witnesses;
   (e) opinions by experts;
   (f) inspection;
   (g) comparative tests or experiments;
   (h) sworn statements in writing (affidavits).
2. The Rules of Procedure shall govern the procedure for taking such evidence. Questioning of witnesses and experts shall be under the control of the Court and be limited to what is necessary.

Article 54
Burden of proof

Without prejudice to Article 24(2) and (3), the burden of the proof of facts shall be on the party relying on those facts.

Article 55
Reversal of burden of proof

1. Without prejudice to Article 24(2) and (3), if the subject-matter of a patent is a process for obtaining a new product, the identical product when produced without the consent of the patent proprietor shall, in the absence of proof to the contrary, be deemed to have been obtained by the patented process.
2. The principle set out in paragraph 1 shall also apply where there is a substantial likelihood that the identical product was made by the patented process and the patent proprietor has been unable, despite reasonable efforts, to determine the process actually used for such identical product.
3. In the adduction of proof to the contrary, the legitimate interests of the defendant in protecting its manufacturing and trade secrets shall be taken into account.

CHAPTER IV

POWERS OF THE COURT

Article 56
The general powers of the Court

1. The Court may impose such measures, procedures and remedies as are laid down in this Agreement and may make its orders subject to conditions, in accordance with the Rules of Procedure.
2. The Court shall take due account of the interest of the parties and shall, before making an order, give any party the opportunity to be heard, unless this is incompatible with the effective enforcement of such order.

Article 57
Court experts

1. Without prejudice to the possibility for the parties to produce expert evidence, the Court may at any time appoint court experts in order to provide expertise for specific aspects of the case. The Court shall provide such expert with all information necessary for the provision of the expert advice.
2. To this end, an indicative list of experts shall be drawn up by the Court in accordance with the Rules of Procedure. That list shall be kept by the Registrar.
3. The court experts shall guarantee independence and impartiality. Rules governing conflicts of interest applicable to judges set out in Article 7 of the Statute shall by analogy apply to court experts.
4. Expert advice given to the Court by court experts shall be made available to the parties which shall have the possibility to comment on it.

Article 58
Protection of confidential information

To protect the trade secrets, personal data or other confidential information of a party to the proceedings or of a third party, or to prevent an abuse of evidence, the Court may order that the collection and use of evidence in proceedings before it be restricted or prohibited or that access to such evidence be restricted to specific persons.

Article 59
Order to produce evidence

1. At the request of a party which has presented reasonably available evidence sufficient to support its claims and has, in substantiating those claims, specified evidence which lies in the control of the opposing party or a third party, the Court may order the opposing party or a third party to present such evidence, subject to the protection of confidential information. Such order shall not result in an obligation of self-incrimination.

2. At the request of a party the Court may order, under the same conditions as specified in paragraph 1, the communication of banking, financial or commercial documents under the control of the opposing party, subject to the protection of confidential information.

Article 60
Order to preserve evidence and to inspect premises

1. At the request of the applicant which has presented reasonably available evidence to support the claim that the patent has been infringed or is about to be infringed the Court may, even before the commencement of proceedings on the merits of the case, order prompt and effective provisional measures to preserve relevant evidence in respect of the alleged infringement, subject to the protection of confidential information.
2. Such measures may include the detailed description, with or without the taking of samples, or the physical seizure of the infringing products, and, in appropriate cases, the materials and implements used in the production and/or distribution of those products and the documents relating thereto.
3. The Court may, even before the commencement of proceedings on the merits of the case, at the request of the applicant who has presented evidence to support the claim that the patent has been infringed or is about to be infringed, order the inspection of premises. Such inspection of premises shall be conducted by a person appointed by the Court in accordance with the Rules of Procedure.
4. At the inspection of the premises the applicant shall not be present itself but may be represented by an independent professional practitioner whose name has to be specified in the Court's order.
5. Measures shall be ordered, if necessary without the other party having been heard, in particular where any delay is likely to cause irreparable harm to the proprietor of the patent, or where there is a demonstrable risk of evidence being destroyed.
6. Where measures to preserve evidence or inspect premises are ordered without the other party in the case having been heard, the parties affected shall be given notice, without delay and at the latest immediately after the execution of the measures. A review, including a right to be heard, shall take place upon request of the parties affected with a view to deciding, within a reasonable period after the notification of the measures, whether the measures are to be modified, revoked or confirmed.
7. The measures to preserve evidence may be subject to the lodging by the applicant of adequate security or an equivalent assurance intended to ensure compensation for any prejudice suffered by the defendant as provided for in paragraph 9.
8. The Court shall ensure that the measures to preserve evidence are revoked or otherwise cease to have effect, at the defendant's request, without prejudice to the damages which may be claimed, if the applicant does not bring, within a period not exceeding 31 calendar days or 20 working days, whichever is the longer, action leading to a decision on the merits of the case before the Court.

9. Where the measures to preserve evidence are revoked, or where they lapse due to any act or omission by the applicant, or where it is subsequently found that there has been no infringement or threat of infringement of the patent, the Court may order the applicant, at the defendant's request, to provide the defendant with appropriate compensation for any damage suffered as a result of those measures.

Article 61
Freezing orders

1. At the request of the applicant which has presented reasonably available evidence to support the claim that the patent has been infringed or is about to be infringed the Court may, even before the commencement of proceedings on the merits of the case, order a party not to remove from its jurisdiction any assets located therein, or not to deal in any assets, whether located within its jurisdiction or not.
2. Article 60(5) to (9) shall apply by analogy to the measures referred to in this Article.

Article 62
Provisional and protective measures

1. The Court may, by way of order, grant injunctions against an alleged infringer or against an intermediary whose services are used by the alleged infringer, intended to prevent any imminent infringement, to prohibit, on a provisional basis and subject, where appropriate, to a recurring penalty payment, the continuation of the alleged infringement or to make such continuation subject to the lodging of guarantees intended to ensure the compensation of the right holder.
2. The Court shall have the discretion to weigh up the interests of the parties and in particular to take into account the potential harm for either of the parties resulting from the granting or the refusal of the injunction.
3. The Court may also order the seizure or delivery up of the products suspected of infringing a patent so as to prevent their entry into, or movement, within the channels of commerce. If the applicant demonstrates circumstances likely to endanger the recovery of damages, the Court may order the precautionary seizure of the movable and immovable property of the alleged infringer, including the blocking of the bank accounts and of other assets of the alleged infringer.
4. The Court may, in respect of the measures referred to in paragraphs 1 and 3, require the applicant to provide any reasonable evidence in order to satisfy itself with a sufficient degree of certainty that the applicant is the right holder and that the applicant's right is being infringed, or that such infringement is imminent.
5. Article 60(5) to (9) shall apply by analogy to the measures referred to in this Article.

Article 63
Permanent injunctions

1. Where a decision is taken finding an infringement of a patent, the Court may grant an injunction against the infringer aimed at prohibiting the continuation of the infringement. The Court may also grant such injunction against an intermediary whose services are being used by a third party to infringe a patent.
2. Where appropriate, non-compliance with the injunction referred to in paragraph 1 shall be subject to a recurring penalty payment payable to the Court.

Article 64
Corrective measures in infringement proceedings

1. Without prejudice to any damages due to the injured party by reason of the infringement, and without compensation of any sort, the Court may order, at the request of the applicant, that appropriate measures be taken with regard to products found to be infringing a patent and, in appropriate cases, with regard to materials and implements principally used in the creation or manufacture of those products.
2. Such measures shall include:
   (a) a declaration of infringement;
   (b) recalling the products from the channels of commerce;
   (c) depriving the product of its infringing property;
   (d) definitively removing the products from the channels of commerce; or
   (e) the destruction of the products and/or of the materials and implements concerned.
3. The Court shall order that those measures be carried out at the expense of the infringer, unless particular reasons are invoked for not doing so.
4. In considering a request for corrective measures pursuant to this Article, the Court shall take into account the need for proportionality between the seriousness of the infringement and the remedies to be ordered, the willingness of the infringer to convert the materials into a non-infringing state, as well as the interests of third parties.

Article 65
Decision on the validity of a patent

1. The Court shall decide on the validity of a patent on the basis of an action for revocation or a counterclaim for revocation.
2. The Court may revoke a patent, either entirely or partly, only on the grounds referred to in Articles 138(1) and 139(2) of the EPC.
3. Without prejudice to Article 138(3) of the EPC, if the grounds for revocation affect the patent only in part, the patent shall be limited by a corresponding amendment of the claims and revoked in part.
4. To the extent that a patent has been revoked it shall be deemed not to have had, from the outset, the effects specified in Articles 64 and 67 of the EPC.

5. Where the Court, in a final decision, revokes a patent, either entirely or partly, it shall send a copy of the decision to the European Patent Office and, with respect to a European patent, to the national patent office of any Contracting Member State concerned.

Article 66
Powers of the Court concerning decisions of the European Patent Office

1. In actions brought under Article 32(1)(i), the Court may exercise any power entrusted on the European Patent Office in accordance with Article 9 of Regulation (EU) No 1257/2012, including the rectification of the Register for unitary patent protection.
2. In actions brought under Article 32(1)(i) the parties shall, by way of derogation from Article 69, bear their own costs.

Article 67
Power to order the communication of information

1. The Court may, in response to a justified and proportionate request of the applicant and in accordance with the Rules of Procedure, order an infringer to inform the applicant of:
    (a) the origin and distribution channels of the infringing products or processes;
    (b) the quantities produced, manufactured, delivered, received or ordered, as well as the price obtained for the infringing products; and
    (c) the identity of any third person involved in the production or distribution of the infringing products or in the use of the infringing process.
2. The Court may, in accordance with the Rules of Procedure, also order any third party who:
    (a) was found in the possession of the infringing products on a commercial scale or to be using an infringing process on a commercial scale;
    (b) was found to be providing on a commercial scale services used in infringing activities; or
    (c) was indicated by the person referred to in points (a) or (b) as being involved in the production, manufacture or distribution of the infringing products or processes or in the provision of the services,

to provide the applicant with the information referred to in paragraph 1.

Article 68
Award of damages

1. The Court shall, at the request of the injured party, order the infringer who knowingly, or with reasonable grounds to know, engaged in a patent infringing activity, to pay the injured party damages appropriate to the harm actually suffered by that party as a result of the infringement.

2. The injured party shall, to the extent possible, be placed in the position it would have been in if no infringement had taken place. The infringer shall not benefit from the infringement. However, damages shall not be punitive.
3. When the Court sets the damages:
   (a) it shall take into account all appropriate aspects, such as the negative economic consequences, including lost profits, which the injured party has suffered, any unfair profits made by the infringer and, in appropriate cases, elements other than economic factors, such as the moral prejudice caused to the injured party by the infringement; or
   (b) as an alternative to point (a), it may, in appropriate cases, set the damages as a lump sum on the basis of elements such as at least the amount of the royalties or fees which would have been due if the infringer had requested authorisation to use the patent in question.
4. Where the infringer did not knowingly, or with reasonable grounds to know, engage in the infringing activity, the Court may order the recovery of profits or the payment of compensation.

Article 69
Legal costs

1. Reasonable and proportionate legal costs and other expenses incurred by the successful party shall, as a general rule, be borne by the unsuccessful party, unless equity requires otherwise, up to a ceiling set in accordance with the Rules of Procedure.
2. Where a party succeeds only in part or in exceptional circumstances, the Court may order that costs be apportioned equitably or that the parties bear their own costs.
3. A party should bear any unnecessary costs it has caused the Court or another party.
4. At the request of the defendant, the Court may order the applicant to provide adequate security for the legal costs and other expenses incurred by the defendant which the applicant may be liable to bear, in particular in the cases referred to in Articles 59 to 62.

Article 70
Court fees

1. Parties to proceedings before the Court shall pay court fees.
2. Court fees shall be paid in advance, unless the Rules of Procedure provide otherwise. Any party which has not paid a prescribed court fee may be excluded from further participation in the proceedings.

Article 71
Legal aid

1. A party who is a natural person and who is unable to meet the costs of the proceedings, either wholly or in part, may at any time apply for legal aid. The conditions for granting of legal aid shall be laid down in the Rules of Procedure.
2. The Court shall decide whether legal aid should be granted in full or in part, or whether it should be refused, in accordance with the Rules of Procedure.
3. On a proposal from the Court, the Administrative Committee shall set the level of legal aid and the rules on bearing the costs thereof.

Article 72
Period of limitation

Without prejudice to Article 24(2) and (3), actions relating to all forms of financial compensation may not be brought more than five years after the date on which the applicant became aware, or had reasonable grounds to become aware, of the last fact justifying the action.

CHAPTER V

APPEALS

Article 73
Appeal

1. An appeal against a decision of the Court of First Instance may be brought before the Court of Appeal by any party which has been unsuccessful, in whole or in part, in its submissions, within two months of the date of the notification of the decision.
2. An appeal against an order of the Court of First Instance may be brought before the Court of Appeal by any party which has been unsuccessful, in whole or in part, in its submissions:
   (a) for the orders referred to in Articles 49(5), 59 to 62 and 67 within 15 calendar days of the notification of the order to the applicant;
   (b) for other orders than the orders referred to in point (a):
      (i) together with the appeal against the decision, or
      (ii) where the Court grants leave to appeal, within 15 days of the notification of the Court's decision to that effect.
3. The appeal against a decision or an order of the Court of First Instance may be based on points of law and matters of fact.

4. New facts and new evidence may only be introduced in accordance with the Rules of Procedure and where the submission thereof by the party concerned could not reasonably have been expected during proceedings before the Court of First Instance.

Article 74
Effects of an appeal

1. An appeal shall not have suspensive effect unless the Court of Appeal decides otherwise at the motivated request of one of the parties. The Rules of Procedure shall guarantee that such a decision is taken without delay.
2. Notwithstanding paragraph 1, an appeal against a decision on actions or counterclaims for revocation and on actions based on Article 32(1)(i) shall always have suspensive effect.
3. An appeal against an order referred to in Articles 49(5), 59 to 62 or 67 shall not prevent the continuation of the main proceedings. However, the Court of First Instance shall not give a decision in the main proceedings before the decision of the Court of Appeal concerning an appealed order has been given.

Article 75
Decision on appeal and referral back

1. If an appeal pursuant to Article 73 is well-founded, the Court of Appeal shall revoke the decision of the Court of First Instance and give a final decision. The Court of Appeal may in exceptional cases and in accordance with the Rules of Procedure refer the case back to the Court of First Instance for decision.
2. Where a case is referred back to the Court of First Instance pursuant to paragraph 1, the Court of First Instance shall be bound by the decision of the Court of Appeal on points of law.

CHAPTER VI

DECISIONS

Article 76
Basis for decisions and right to be heard

1. The Court shall decide in accordance with the requests submitted by the parties and shall not award more than is requested.
2. Decisions on the merits may only be based on grounds, facts and evidence, which were submitted by the parties or introduced into the procedure by an order of the Court and on which the parties have had an opportunity to present their comments.
3. The Court shall evaluate evidence freely and independently.

Article 77
Formal requirements

1. Decisions and orders of the Court shall be reasoned and shall be given in writing in accordance with the Rules of Procedure.
2. Decisions and orders of the Court shall be delivered in the language of proceedings.

Article 78
Decisions of the Court and dissenting opinions

1. Decisions and orders of the Court shall be taken by a majority of the panel, in accordance with the Statute. In case of equal votes, the vote of the presiding judge shall prevail.
2. In exceptional circumstances, any judge of the panel may express a dissenting opinion separately from the decision of the Court.

Article 79
Settlement

The parties may, at any time in the course of proceedings, conclude their case by way of settlement, which shall be confirmed by a decision of the Court. A patent may not be revoked or limited by way of settlement.

Article 80
Publication of decisions

The Court may order, at the request of the applicant and at the expense of the infringer, appropriate measures for the dissemination of information concerning the Court's decision, including displaying the decision and publishing it in full or in part in public media.

Article 81
Rehearing

1. A request for rehearing after a final decision of the Court may exceptionally be granted by the Court of Appeal in the following circumstances:
   (a) on discovery of a fact by the party requesting the rehearing, which is of such a nature as to be a decisive factor and which, when the decision was given, was unknown to the party requesting the rehearing; such request may only be granted on the basis of an act which was held, by a final decision of a national court, to constitute a criminal offence; or
   (b) in the event of a fundamental procedural defect, in particular when a defendant who did not appear before the Court was not served with the document initiating the proceedings or an equivalent document in sufficient time and in such a way as to enable him to arrange for the defence.

2. A request for a rehearing shall be filed within 10 years of the date of the decision but not later than two months from the date of the discovery of the new fact or of the procedural defect. Such request shall not have suspensive effect unless the Court of Appeal decides otherwise.
3. If the request for a rehearing is well-founded, the Court of Appeal shall set aside, in whole or in part, the decision under review and re-open the proceedings for a new trial and decision, in accordance with the Rules of Procedure.
4. Persons using patents which are the subject-matter of a decision under review and who act in good faith should be allowed to continue using such patents.

Article 82
Enforcement of decisions and orders

1. Decisions and orders of the Court shall be enforceable in any Contracting Member State. An order for the enforcement of a decision shall be appended to the decision by the Court.
2. Where appropriate, the enforcement of a decision may be subject to the provision of security or an equivalent assurance to ensure compensation for any damage suffered, in particular in the case of injunctions.
3. Without prejudice to this Agreement and the Statute, enforcement procedures shall be governed by the law of the Contracting Member State where the enforcement takes place. Any decision of the Court shall be enforced under the same conditions as a decision given in the Contracting Member State where the enforcement takes place.
4. If a party does not comply with the terms of an order of the Court, that party may be sanctioned with a recurring penalty payment payable to the Court. The individual penalty shall be proportionate to the importance of the order to be enforced and shall be without prejudice to the party's right to claim damages or security.

PART IV
TRANSITIONAL PROVISIONS

Article 83
Transitional regime

1. During a transitional period of seven years after the date of entry into force of this Agreement, an action for infringement or for revocation of a European patent or an action for infringement or for declaration of invalidity of a supplementary protection certificate issued for a product protected by a European patent may still be brought before national courts or other competent national authorities.
2. An action pending before a national court at the end of the transitional period shall not be affected by the expiry of this period.

3. Unless an action has already been brought before the Court, a proprietor of or an applicant for a European patent granted or applied for prior to the end of the transitional period under paragraph 1 and, where applicable, paragraph 5, as well as a holder of a supplementary protection certificate issued for a product protected by a European patent, shall have the possibility to opt out from the exclusive competence of the Court. To this end they shall notify their opt-out to the Registry by the latest one month before expiry of the transitional period. The opt-out shall take effect upon its entry into the register.
4. Unless an action has already been brought before a national court, proprietors of or applicants for European patents or holders of supplementary protection certificates issued for a product protected by a European patent who made use of the opt-out in accordance with paragraph 3 shall be entitled to withdraw their opt-out at any moment. In this event they shall notify the Registry accordingly. The withdrawal of the opt-out shall take effect upon its entry into the register.
5. Five years after the entry into force of this Agreement, the Administrative Committee shall carry out a broad consultation with the users of the patent system and a survey on the number of European patents and supplementary protection certificates issued for products protected by European patents with respect to which actions for infringement or for revocation or declaration of invalidity are still brought before the national courts pursuant to paragraph 1, the reasons for this and the implications thereof. On the basis of this consultation and an opinion of the Court, the Administrative Committee may decide to prolong the transitional period by up to seven years.

PART V
FINAL PROVISIONS

Article 84
Signature, ratification and accession

1. This Agreement shall be open for signature by any Member State on 19 February 2013.
2. This Agreement shall be subject to ratification in accordance with the respective constitutional requirements of the Member States. Instruments of ratification shall be deposited with the General Secretariat of the Council of the European Union (hereinafter referred to as 'the depositary').
3. Each Member State having signed this Agreement shall notify the European Commission of its ratification of the Agreement at the time of the deposit of its ratification instrument pursuant to Article 18(3) of Regulation (EU) No 1257/2012.
4. This Agreement shall be open to accession by any Member State. Instruments of accession shall be deposited with the depositary.

Article 85
Functions of the depositary

1. The depositary shall draw up certified true copies of this Agreement and shall transmit them to the governments of all signatory or acceding Member States.
2. The depositary shall notify the governments of the signatory or acceding Member States of:
   (a) any signature;
   (b) the deposit of any instrument of ratification or accession;
   (c) the date of entry into force of this Agreement.
3. The depositary shall register this Agreement with the Secretariat of the United Nations.

Article 86
Duration of the Agreement

This Agreement shall be of unlimited duration.

Article 87
Revision

1. Either seven years after the entry into force of this Agreement or once 2000 infringement cases have been decided by the Court, whichever is the later point in time, and if necessary at regular intervals thereafter, a broad consultation with the users of the patent system shall be carried out by the Administrative Committee on the functioning, efficiency and cost-effectiveness of the Court and on the trust and confidence of users of the patent system in the quality of the Court's decisions. On the basis of this consultation and an opinion of the Court, the Administrative Committee may decide to revise this Agreement with a view to improving the functioning of the Court.
2. The Administrative Committee may amend this Agreement to bring it into line with an international treaty relating to patents or Union law.
3. A decision of the Administrative Committee taken on the basis of paragraphs 1 and 2 shall not take effect if a Contracting Member State declares within twelve months of the date of the decision, on the basis of its relevant internal decision-making procedures, that it does not wish to be bound by the decision. In this case, a Review Conference of the Contracting Member States shall be convened.

Article 88
Languages of the Agreement

1. This Agreement is drawn up in a single original in the English, French and German languages, each text being equally authentic.
2. The texts of this Agreement drawn up in official languages of Contracting Member States other than those specified in paragraph 1 shall, if they have been approved by the Administrative Committee, be considered as official texts. In the event of divergences between the various texts, the texts referred to in paragraph 1 shall prevail.

Article 89
Entry into force

1. This Agreement shall enter into force on 1 January 2014 or on the first day of the fourth month after the deposit of the thirteenth instrument of ratification or accession in accordance with Article 84, including the three Member States in which the highest number of European patents had effect in the year preceding the year in which the signature of the Agreement takes place or on the first day of the fourth month after the date of entry into force of the amendments to Regulation (EU) No 1215/2012 concerning its relationship with this Agreement, whichever is the latest.
2. Any ratification or accession after the entry into force of this Agreement shall take effect on the first day of the fourth month after the deposit of the instrument of ratification or accession.

In witness whereof the undersigned, being duly authorised thereto, have signed this Agreement,

Done at Brussels on 19 February 2013 in English, French and German, all three texts being equally authentic, in a single copy which shall be deposited in the archives of the General Secretariat of the Council of the European Union.

(1) Regulation (EU) No 1257/2012 of the European Parliament and of the Council of 17 December 2012 implementing enhanced cooperation in the area of the creation of unitary patent protection (OJ L361, 31.12.2012, p. 1) including any subsequent amendments.
(2) Regulation (EU) No 1215/2012 of the European Parliament and of the Council of 12 December 2012 on jurisdiction and the recognition and enforcement of judgments in civil and commercial matters (OJ L351, 20.12.2012, p. 1) including any subsequent amendments.
(3) Regulation (EC) No 469/2009 of the European Parliament and of the Council of 6 May 2009 concerning the supplementary protection certificate for medicinal products (OJ L152, 16.6.2009, p. 1) including any subsequent amendments.
(4) Regulation (EC) No 1610/96 of the European Parliament and of the Council of 23 July 1996 concerning the creation of a supplementary certificate for plant protection products (OJ L198, 8.8.1996, p. 30) including any subsequent amendments.
(5) Regulation (EC) No 593/2008 of the European Parliament and of the Council of 17 June 2008 on the law applicable to contractual obligations (Rome I) (OJ L177, 4.7.2008, p. 6) including any subsequent amendments.
(6) Regulation (EC) No 864/2007 of the European Parliament and of the Council of 11 July 2007 on the law applicable to non-contractual obligations (Rome II) (OJ L199, 31.7.2007, p. 40) including any subsequent amendments.

(7) Council Regulation (EU) No 1260/2012 of 17 December 2012 implementing enhanced cooperation in the area of the creation of unitary patent protection with regard to the applicable translation arrangements (OJ L361, 31.12.2012, p. 89) including any subsequent amendments.

(8) Directive 2001/82/EC of the European Parliament and of the Council of 6 November 2001 on the Community code relating to veterinary medicinal products (OJ L311, 28.11.2001, p. 1) including any subsequent amendments.

(9) Directive 2001/83/EC of the European Parliament and of the Council of 6 November 2001 on the Community code relating to medicinal products for human use (OJ L311, 28.11.2001, p. 67) including any subsequent amendments.

(10) International Civil Aviation Organization (ICAO), 'Chicago Convention', Document 7300/9 (9th edition, 2006).

(11) Council Regulation (EC) No 2100/94 of 27 July 1994 on Community plant variety rights (OJ L227, 1.9.1994, p. 1) including any subsequent amendments.

(12) Directive 2009/24/EC of the European Parliament and of the Council of 23 April 2009 on the legal protection of computer programs (OJ L111, 5.5.2009, p. 16) including any subsequent amendments.

(13) Directive 98/44/EC of the European Parliament and of the Council of 6 July 1998 on the legal protection of biotechnological inventions (OJ L213, 30.7.1998, p. 13) including any subsequent amendments.

(14) Convention on jurisdiction and the recognition and enforcement of judgments in civil and commercial matters, done at Lugano on 30 October 2007, including any subsequent amendments.

ANNEX I

STATUTE OF THE UNIFIED PATENT COURT

Article 1
Scope of the Statute

This Statute contains institutional and financial arrangements for the Unified Patent Court as established under Article 1 of the Agreement.

CHAPTER I

JUDGES

Article 2
Eligibility of judges

1. Any person who is a national of a Contracting Member State and fulfils the conditions set out in Article 15 of the Agreement and in this Statute may be appointed as a judge.
2. Judges shall have a good command of at least one official language of the European Patent Office.
3. Experience with patent litigation which has to be proven for the appointment pursuant to Article 15(1) of the Agreement may be acquired by training under Article 11(4)(a) of this Statute.

Article 3
Appointment of judges

1. Judges shall be appointed pursuant to the procedure set out in Article 16 of the Agreement.
2. Vacancies shall be publicly advertised and shall indicate the relevant eligibility criteria as set out in Article 2. The Advisory Committee shall give an opinion on candidates' suitability to perform the duties of a judge of the Court. The opinion shall comprise a list of most suitable candidates. The list shall contain at least twice as many candidates as there are vacancies. Where necessary, the Advisory Committee may recommend that, prior to the decision on the appointment, a candidate judge receive training in patent litigation pursuant to Article 11(4)(a).
3. When appointing judges, the Administrative Committee shall ensure the best legal and technical expertise and a balanced composition of the Court on as broad a geographical basis as possible among nationals of the Contracting Member States.

4. The Administrative Committee shall appoint as many judges as are needed for the proper functioning of the Court. The Administrative Committee shall initially appoint the necessary number of judges for setting up at least one panel in each of the divisions of the Court of First Instance and at least two panels in the Court of Appeal.
5. The decision of the Administrative Committee appointing full-time or part-time legally qualified judges and full-time technically qualified judges shall state the instance of the Court and/or the division of the Court of First Instance for which each judge is appointed and the field(s) of technology for which a technically qualified judge is appointed.
6. Part-time technically qualified judges shall be appointed as judges of the Court and shall be included in the Pool of Judges on the basis of their specific qualifications and experience. The appointment of these judges to the Court shall ensure that all fields of technology are covered.

Article 4
Judges' term of office

1. Judges shall be appointed for a term of six years, beginning on the date laid down in the instrument of appointment. They may be re-appointed.
2. In the absence of any provision regarding the date, the term shall begin on the date of the instrument of appointment.

Article 5
Appointment of the members of the Advisory Committee

1. Each Contracting Member State shall propose a member of the Advisory Committee who fulfils the requirements set out in Article 14(2) of the Agreement.
2. The members of the Advisory Committee shall be appointed by the Administrative Committee acting by common accord.

Article 6
Oath

Before taking up their duties judges shall, in open court, take an oath to perform their duties impartially and conscientiously and to preserve the secrecy of the deliberations of the Court.

Article 7
Impartiality

1. Immediately after taking their oath, judges shall sign a declaration by which they solemnly undertake that, both during and after their term of office, they shall respect the obligations arising therefrom, in particular the duty to behave with integrity and discretion as regards the acceptance, after they have ceased to hold office, of certain appointments or benefits.

2. Judges may not take part in the proceedings of a case in which they:
    (a) have taken part as adviser;
    (b) have been a party or have acted for one of the parties;
    (c) have been called upon to pronounce as a member of a court, tribunal, board of appeal, arbitration or mediation panel, a commission of inquiry or in any other capacity;
    (d) have a personal or financial interest in the case or in relation to one of the parties; or
    (e) are related to one of the parties or the representatives of the parties by family ties.
3. If, for some special reason, a judge considers that he or she should not take part in the judgement or examination of a particular case, that judge shall so inform the President of the Court of Appeal accordingly or, in the case of judges of the Court of First Instance, the President of the Court of First Instance. If, for some special reason, the President of the Court of Appeal or, in the case of judges of the Court of First Instance, the President of the Court of First Instance considers that a judge should not sit or make submissions in a particular case, the President of the Court of Appeal or the President of the Court of First Instance shall justify this in writing and notify the judge concerned accordingly.
4. Any party to an action may object to a judge taking part in the proceedings on any of the grounds listed in paragraph 2 or where the judge is suspected, with good reason, of partiality.
5. Any difficulty arising as to the application of this Article shall be settled by decision of the Presidium, in accordance with the Rules of Procedure. The judge concerned shall be heard but shall not take part in the deliberations.

Article 8
Immunity of judges

1. The judges shall be immune from legal proceedings. After they have ceased to hold office, they shall continue to enjoy immunity in respect of acts performed by them in relation to their official capacity.
2. The Presidium may waive the immunity.
3. Where immunity has been waived and criminal proceedings are instituted against a judge, that judge shall be tried, in any of the Contracting Member States, only by the court competent to judge the members of the highest national judiciary.
4. The Protocol on the privileges and immunities of the European Union shall apply to the judges of the Court, without prejudice to the provisions relating to immunity from legal proceedings of judges which are set out in this Statute.

Article 9
End of duties

1. Apart from replacement after expiry of a judge's term pursuant to Article 4, or death, the duties of a judge shall end when that judge resigns.
2. Where a judge resigns, the letter of resignation shall be addressed to the President of the Court of Appeal or, in the case of judges of the Court of First Instance, the President of the Court of First Instance for transmission to the Chairman of the Administrative Committee.
3. Save where Article 10 applies, a judge shall continue to hold office until that judge's successor takes up his or her duties.
4. Any vacancy shall by filled by the appointment of a new judge for the remainder of his or her predecessor's term.

Article 10
Removal from office

1. A judge may be deprived of his or her office or of other benefits only if the Presidium decides that that judge no longer fulfils the requisite conditions or meets the obligations arising from his or her office. The judge concerned shall be heard but shall not take part in the deliberations.
2. The Registrar of the Court shall communicate this decision to the Chairman of the Administrative Committee.
3. In the case of a decision depriving a judge of his or her office, a vacancy shall arise upon that notification.

Article 11
Training

1. Appropriate and regular training of judges shall be provided for within the training framework set up under Article 19 of the Agreement. The Presidium shall adopt Training Regulations ensuring the implementation and overall coherence of the training framework.
2. The training framework shall provide a platform for the exchange of expertise and a forum for discussion, in particular by:
   (a) organising courses, conferences, seminars, workshops and symposia;
   (b) cooperating with international organisations and education institutes in the field of intellectual property; and
   (c) promoting and supporting further vocational training.
3. An annual work programme and training guidelines shall be drawn up, which shall include for each judge an annual training plan identifying that judge's main training needs in accordance with the Training Regulations.
4. The training framework shall in addition:
   (a) ensure appropriate training for candidate-judges and newly appointed judges of the Court;
   (b) support projects aimed at facilitating cooperation between representatives, patent attorneys and the Court.

Article 12
Remuneration

The Administrative Committee shall set the remuneration of the President of the Court of Appeal, the President of the Court of First Instance, the judges, the Registrar, the Deputy-Registrar and the staff.

CHAPTER II

ORGANISATIONAL PROVISIONS

SECTION 1
COMMON PROVISIONS

Article 13
President of the Court of Appeal

1. The President of the Court of Appeal shall be elected by all judges of the Court of Appeal for a term of three years, from among their number. The President of the Court of Appeal may be re-elected twice.
2. The elections of the President of the Court of Appeal shall be by secret ballot. A judge obtaining an absolute majority shall be elected. If no judge obtains an absolute majority, a second ballot shall be held and the judge obtaining the most votes shall be elected.
3. The President of the Court of Appeal shall direct the judicial activities and the administration of the Court of Appeal and chair the Court of Appeal sitting as a full Court.
4. If the office of the President of the Court of Appeal falls vacant before the date of expiry of his or her term, a successor shall be elected for the remainder thereof.

Article 14
President of the Court of First Instance

1. The President of the Court of First Instance shall be elected by all judges of the Court of First Instance who are full-time judges, for a term of three years, from among their number. The President of the Court of First Instance may be re-elected twice.
2. The first President of the Court of First Instance shall be a national of the Contracting Member State hosting the seat of the central division.
3. The President of the Court of First Instance shall direct the judicial activities and the administration of the Court of First Instance.
4. Article 13(2) and (4), shall by analogy apply to the President of the Court of First Instance.

Article 15
Presidium

1. The Presidium shall be composed of the President of the Court of Appeal, who shall act as chairperson, the President of the Court of First Instance, two judges of the Court of Appeal elected from among their number, three judges of the Court of First Instance who are full-time judges of the Court elected from among their number, and the Registrar as a non-voting member.
2. The Presidium shall exercise its duties in accordance with this Statute. It may, without prejudice to its own responsibility, delegate certain tasks to one of its members.
3. The Presidium shall be responsible for the management of the Court and shall in particular:
   (a) draw up proposals for the amendment of the Rules of Procedure in accordance with Article 41 of the Agreement and proposals regarding the Financial Regulations of the Court;
   (b) prepare the annual budget, the annual accounts and the annual report of the Court and submit them to the Budget Committee;
   (c) establish the guidelines for the training programme for judges and supervise the implementation thereof;
   (d) take decisions on the appointment and removal of the Registrar and the Deputy-Registrar;
   (e) lay down the rules governing the Registry including the sub-registries;
   (f) give an opinion in accordance with Article 83(5) of the Agreement.
4. Decisions of the Presidium referred to in Articles 7, 8, 10 and 22 shall be taken without the participation of the Registrar.
5. The Presidium can take valid decisions only when all members are present or duly represented. Decisions shall be taken by a majority of the votes.

Article 16
Staff

1. The officials and other servants of the Court shall have the task of assisting the President of the Court of Appeal, the President of the Court of First Instance, the judges and the Registrar. They shall be responsible to the Registrar, under the authority of the President of the Court of Appeal and the President of the Court of First Instance.
2. The Administrative Committee shall establish the Staff Regulations of officials and other servants of the Court.

Article 17
Judicial vacations

1. After consulting the Presidium, the President of the Court of Appeal shall establish the duration of judicial vacations and the rules on observing official holidays.

2. During the period of judicial vacations, the functions of the President of the Court of Appeal and of the President of the Court of First Instance may be exercised by any judge invited by the respective President to that effect. In cases of urgency, the President of the Court of Appeal may convene the judges.
3. The President of the Court of Appeal or the President of the Court of First Instance may, in proper circumstances, grant leave of absence to respectively judges of the Court of Appeal or judges of the Court of First Instance.

SECTION 2
THE COURT OF FIRST INSTANCE

Article 18
Setting up and discontinuance of a local or regional division

1. A request from one or more Contracting Member States for the setting up of a local or regional division shall be addressed to the Chairman of the Administrative Committee. It shall indicate the seat of the local or regional division.
2. The decision of the Administrative Committee setting up a local or regional division shall indicate the number of judges for the division concerned and shall be public.
3. The Administrative Committee shall decide to discontinue a local or regional division at the request of the Contracting Member State hosting the local division or the Contracting Member States participating in the regional division. The decision to discontinue a local or regional division shall state the date after which no new cases may be brought before the division and the date on which the division will cease to exist.
4. As from the date on which a local or regional division ceases to exist, the judges assigned to that local or regional division shall be assigned to the central division, and cases still pending before that local or regional division together with the sub-registry and all of its documentation shall be transferred to the central division.

Article 19
Panels

1. The allocation of judges and the assignment of cases within a division to its panels shall be governed by the Rules of Procedure. One judge of the panel shall be designated as the presiding judge, in accordance with the Rules of Procedure.
2. The panel may delegate, in accordance with the Rules of Procedure, certain functions to one or more of its judges.

3. A standing judge for each division to hear urgent cases may be designated in accordance with the Rules of Procedure.
4. In cases where a single judge in accordance with Article 8(7) of the Agreement, or a standing judge, in accordance with paragraph 3 of this Article, hears a case that judge shall carry out all functions of a panel.
5. One judge of the panel shall act as Rapporteur, in accordance with the Rules of Procedure.

Article 20
Pool of Judges

1. A list with the names of the judges included in the Pool of Judges shall be drawn up by the Registrar. In relation to each judge, the list shall at least indicate the linguistic skills, the field of technology and experience of, as well as the cases previously handled by, that judge.
2. A request addressed to the President of the Court of First Instance to assign a judge from the Pool of Judges shall indicate, in particular, the subject-matter of the case, the official language of the European Patent Office used by the judges of the panel, the language of the proceedings and the field of technology required.

SECTION 3
THE COURT OF APPEAL

Article 21
Panels

1. The allocation of judges and the assignment of cases to panels shall be governed by the Rules of Procedure. One judge of the panel shall be appointed as the presiding judge, in accordance with the Rules of Procedure.
2. When a case is of exceptional importance, and in particular when the decision may affect the unity and consistency of the case law of the Court, the Court of Appeal may decide, on the basis of a proposal from the presiding judge, to refer the case to the full Court.
3. The panel may delegate, in accordance with the Rules of Procedure, certain functions to one or more of its judges.
4. One judge of the panel shall act as Rapporteur, in accordance with the Rules of Procedure.

SECTION 4
THE REGISTRY

Article 22
Appointment and removal from office of the Registrar

1. The Presidium shall appoint the Registrar of the Court for a term of six years. The Registrar may be re-appointed.
2. Two weeks before the date fixed for appointing the Registrar, the President of the Court of Appeal shall inform the Presidium of the applications which have been submitted for the post.
3. Before taking up his or her duties, the Registrar shall take oath before the Presidium to perform the duties of the Registrar impartially and conscientiously.
4. The Registrar may be removed from office only if the Registrar no longer meets the obligations arising from his or her office. The Presidium shall take its decision after having heard the Registrar.
5. If the office of the Registrar falls vacant before the date of expiry of the term thereof, the Presidium shall appoint a new Registrar for a term of six years.
6. If the Registrar is absent or prevented from attending or where such post is vacant, the President of the Court of Appeal after having consulted the Presidium shall designate a member of the staff of the Court to carry out the duties of the Registrar.

Article 23
Duties of the Registrar

1. The Registrar shall assist the Court, the President of the Court of Appeal, the President of the Court of First Instance and the judges in the performance of their functions. The Registrar shall be responsible for the organisation and activities of the Registry under the authority of the President of the Court of Appeal.
2. The Registrar shall in particular be responsible for:
   (a) keeping the register which shall include records of all cases before the Court;
   (b) keeping and administering lists drawn up in accordance with Articles 18, 48(3) and 57(2) of the Agreement;
   (c) keeping and publishing a list of notifications and withdrawals of opt-outs in accordance with Article 83 of the Agreement;
   (d) publishing the decisions of the Court, subject to the protection of confidential information;
   (e) publishing annual reports with statistical data; and
   (f) ensuring that the information on opt-outs in accordance with Article 83 of the Agreement is notified to the European Patent Office.

Article 24
Keeping of the register

1. Detailed rules for keeping the register of the Court shall be prescribed in the Rules governing the Registry, adopted by the Presidium.
2. The rules on access to documents of the Registry shall be provided for in the Rules of Procedure.

Article 25
Sub-registries and Deputy-Registrar

1. A Deputy-Registrar shall be appointed for a term of six years by the Presidium. The Deputy-Registrar may be re-appointed.
2. Article 22(2) to (6) shall apply by analogy.
3. The Deputy-Registrar shall be responsible for the organisation and activities of sub-registries under the authority of the Registrar and the President of the Court of First Instance. The duties of the Deputy-Registrar shall in particular include:
   (a) keeping records of all cases before the Court of First Instance;
   (b) notifying every case before the Court of First Instance to the Registry.
4. The Deputy-Registrar shall also provide administrative and secretarial assistance to the divisions of the Court of First Instance.

CHAPTER III

FINANCIAL PROVISIONS

Article 26
Budget

1. The budget shall be adopted by the Budget Committee on a proposal from the Presidium. It shall be drawn up in accordance with the generally accepted accounting principles laid down in the Financial Regulations, established in accordance with Article 33.
2. Within the budget, the Presidium may, in accordance with the Financial Regulations, transfer funds between the various headings or subheadings.
3. The Registrar shall be responsible for the implementation of the budget in accordance with the Financial Regulations.
4. The Registrar shall annually make a statement on the accounts of the preceding financial year relating to the implementation of the budget which shall be approved by the Presidium.

Article 27
Authorisation for expenditure

1. The expenditure entered in the budget shall be authorised for the duration of one accounting period unless the Financial Regulations provide otherwise.
2. In accordance with the Financial Regulations, any appropriations, other than those relating to staff costs, which are unexpended at the end of the accounting period may be carried forward, but not beyond the end of the following accounting period.
3. Appropriations shall be set out under different headings according to type and purpose of the expenditure, and subdivided, to the extent necessary, in accordance with the Financial Regulations.

Article 28
Appropriations for unforeseeable expenditure

1. The budget of the Court may include appropriations for unforeseeable expenditure.
2. The employment of these appropriations by the Court shall be subject to the prior approval of the Budget Committee.

Article 29
Accounting period

The accounting period shall commence on 1 January and end on 31 December.

Article 30
Preparation of the budget

The Presidium shall submit the draft budget of the Court to the Budget Committee no later than the date prescribed in the Financial Regulations.

Article 31
Provisional budget

1. If, at the beginning of the accounting period, the budget has not been adopted by the Budget Committee, expenditure may be effected on a monthly basis per heading or other division of the budget, in accordance with the Financial Regulations, up to one-twelfth of the budget appropriations for the preceding accounting period, provided that the appropriations thus made available to the Presidium do not exceed one-twelfth of those provided for in the draft budget.
2. The Budget Committee may, subject to the observance of the other provisions laid down in paragraph 1, authorise expenditure in excess of one-twelfth of the budget appropriations for the preceding accounting period.

Article 32
Auditing of accounts

1. The annual financial statements of the Court shall be examined by independent auditors. The auditors shall be appointed and if necessary dismissed by the Budget Committee.
2. The audit, which shall be based on professional auditing standards and shall take place, if necessary, in situ, shall ascertain that the budget has been implemented in a lawful and proper manner and that the financial administration of the Court has been conducted in accordance with the principles of economy and sound financial management. The auditors shall draw up a report after the end of each accounting period containing a signed audit opinion.
3. The Presidium shall submit to the Budget Committee the annual financial statements of the Court and the annual budget implementation statement for the preceding accounting period, together with the auditors' report.
4. The Budget Committee shall approve the annual accounts together with the auditors' report and shall discharge the Presidium in respect of the implementation of the budget.

Article 33
Financial Regulations

1. The Financial Regulations shall be adopted by the Administrative Committee. They shall be amended by the Administrative Committee on a proposal from the Court.
2. The Financial Regulations shall lay down in particular:
   (a) arrangements relating to the establishment and implementation of the budget and for the rendering and auditing of accounts;
   (b) the method and procedure whereby the payments and contributions, including the initial financial contributions provided for in Article 37 of the Agreement are to be made available to the Court;
   (c) the rules concerning the responsibilities of authorising and accounting officers and the arrangements for their supervision; and
   (d) the generally accepted accounting principles on which the budget and the annual financial statements are to be based.

CHAPTER IV

PROCEDURAL PROVISIONS

Article 34
Secrecy of deliberations

The deliberations of the Court shall be and shall remain secret.

Article 35
Decisions

1. When a panel sits in composition of an even number of judges, decisions of the Court shall be taken by a majority of the panel. In case of equal vote, the vote of the presiding judge shall prevail.
2. In the event of one of the judges of a panel being prevented from attending, a judge from another panel may be called upon to sit in accordance with the Rules of Procedure.
3. In cases where this Statute provides that the Court of Appeal shall take a decision sitting as a full court, such decision shall be valid only if it is taken by at least 3/4 of the judges comprising the full court.
4. Decisions of the Court shall contain the names of the judges deciding the case.
5. Decisions shall be signed by the judges deciding the case, by the Registrar for decisions of the Court of Appeal, and by the Deputy-Registrar for decisions of the Court of First Instance. They shall be read in open court.

Article 36
Dissenting opinions

A dissenting opinion expressed separately by a judge of a panel in accordance with Article 78 of the Agreement shall be reasoned, given in writing and shall be signed by the judge expressing this opinion.

Article 37
Decision by default

1. At the request of a party to an action, a decision by default may be given in accordance with the Rules of Procedure, where the other party, after having been served with a document instituting proceedings or with an equivalent document, fails to file written submissions in defence or fails to appear at the oral hearing. An objection may be lodged against that decision within one month of it being notified to the party against which the default decision has been given.
2. The objection shall not have the effect of staying enforcement of the decision by default unless the Court decides otherwise.

Article 38
Questions referred to the Court of Justice of the European Union

1. The procedures established by the Court of Justice of the European Union for referrals for preliminary rulings within the European Union shall apply.
2. Whenever the Court of First Instance or the Court of Appeal has decided to refer to the Court of Justice of the European Union a question of interpretation of the Treaty on European Union or of the Treaty on the Functioning of the European Union or a question on the validity or interpretation of acts of the institutions of the European Union, it shall stay its proceedings.

[1] The classification into eight sections (A–H) is based on the International Patent Classification of the World Intellectual Property Organization (www.wipo.int/classifications/ipc/en).

ANNEX II

DISTRIBUTION OF CASES WITHIN THE CENTRAL DIVISION[1]

LONDON Section	PARIS Seat President's Office	MUNICH Section
(A) Human necessities	(B) Performing operations, transporting	(F) Mechanical engineering, lighting, heating, weapons, blasting
(C) Chemistry, metallurgy	(D) Textiles, paper	
	(E) Fixed constructions	
	(G) Physics	
	(H) Electricity	

INDEX